A Master Class with Warren Buffett and Charlie Munger

The Q&A Sessions of the Berkshire Hathaway Inc.
Shareholders Meeting

2017

by

Eben Otuteye, PhD
and
Mohammad Siddiquee, PhD

I0492383

Cover Design: Nancy Wood, University of New Brunswick Media Services

ISBN 13: 978-1983578625
ISBN 10: 1983578622

Disclaimer: This book is for educational purposes only. These notes are not verified or approved by Warren Buffett, Charlie Munger, nor by any director or officer of Berkshire Hathaway Inc. We relied primarily on our handwritten notes from the meeting. This publication is not meant to offer investment advice. No part of the information in this book should be considered a recommendation to purchase or sell any security.

Authors in front of Kiewit Plaza in Omaha
Photo credit: Alim Mirza

"Lose money for the firm and I will be understanding; lose a shred of reputation for the firm and I will be ruthless."
Warren Buffett

Table of Contents

Preface

There is no question that Warren Buffett and Charlie Munger are investment legends of our time. Over the years they have demonstrated that they are not only great investment and business managers but that they are also sages with tremendous amount of worldly wisdom that will help people to navigate life successfully.

There are countless books written about Warren Buffett and Charlie Munger's investment style and investment success. However, there are very few sources to get their thoughts and words as directly expressed by them. Usually, you get those from interviews, newspaper or magazine articles, or more directly from the annual letter to shareholders. One rich, but generally overlooked and not well-dcoumented source of Buffett-Munger wisdom is the question and answer sessions of the annual general meeting.

The Annual General Meeting of Berkshire Hathaway shareholders is one forum where Warren Buffett and Charlie Munger generously share their knowledge and insights on various topics. Thus, if anyone is looking for a shortcut to Buffett-Munger wisdom in investment, business, and life, the best advice is to go the Berkshire Shareholders Meeting or to get the transcript of the question and answer sessions – and is that what you get from this book.

Motivation for Writing the Master Class Series

As professors of Finance who have taken a number of business courses and now teach a number of courses in Investments and Personal Financial Planning, we have felt and lived with a sense of dissatisfaction with the traditional academic models of investment and the methods of teaching for a long time. After we discovered the works of Ben Graham and the practice of investment by Warren Buffett, Charlie Munger and several other value investors, it became clear to us that the traditional finance curriculum in academia is shortchanging our students (the next generation) in a big way. We then took it upon ourselves to do a thorough study of the investment philosophy and practices of legendary value investors, especially Warren Buffett and Charlie Munger. In the process, we came know about this annual event called the Berkshire Hathaway shareholders meeting.

Being relatively new to Berkshire Hathaway shareholders meeting, we thought we could prepare ourselves by reading some material on it. Apart from Warren Buffett's letters to shareholders and the Berkshire annual reports, the main resource we consulted was the book *Pilgrimage to Warren Buffett's Omaha* by Jeff Mathews, which gave us quite a good orientation. In the process, we realized that there's no reliable and readily available source to access the actual Q&A sessions of past shareholders meeting. It is our opinion that majority of those who attend the meeting are keen and teachable learners who will appreciate a reference source to review the questions and answers of the meeting. Hence, the motivation for this book. We hope both Warren Buffett and Charlie Munger will stick around for a while and maintain this format of the annual meeting in order to give us the opportunity to continue to tap into their insight and wisdom.

Another motivation for the book is that since both of us came to know about Warren Buffett and Charlie Munger rather late, we figured the way to make up for this is to introduce our students very early in their business education to the ideas of these legendary investors. Writing this series is our way of contributing to the efforts of those who are committed to spreading the word about the right way to invest, to think about money, and to manage businesses. We hope to use this *Master Class* series as the means to disseminate the ideas of Warren Buffett and Charlie Munger as directly enunciated and articulated by them. We believe it will be a great service not only to the investment community but to society in general.

Eben Otuteye
Mohammad Siddiquee
April 2018

About the Title of the Book

On May 6, 2014, Bill Gates posted a blog[1] that began:

"In the arts, a master class is a group lesson with an acknowledged expert—a chance for students to hear from an undisputed master and to improve their work by being exposed to the best.

This last weekend, I joined almost forty thousand other 'students' to attend the master class for investors that is the Berkshire Hathaway annual meeting."

That blog resonated immediately with us and we decided to use the title of the blog as the title of this book. The Berkshire Hathaway AGM is indeed a master class with legends.

Accuracy of Content

As those who attend the AGM are aware, part of the protocol is that no electronic recording equipment is permitted. In previous editions, the entire content of the book was compiled solely from handwritten notes taken at the meeting. We then consulted a number of other attendants to cross-check our notes. However, since 2016, Yahoo Finance has been livestreaming and recording the event and that has made it easier for us to check the accuracy of our notes.

Although we tried to transcribe what was said as accurately as possible, we weren't able to make a verbatim copy. A

---

[1] http://www.gatesnotes.com/About-Bill-Gates/Master-Class-with-Warren-Buffett-Berkshire-Hathaway-Annual-Meeting-2014

number of expressions are paraphrases of what was actually said. However, we've made every effort to preserve the sense and meaning of what was said. While our words are not always identical to notes taken by others, we are satisfied that the content is an accurate representation of what was said. Of course, the punctuation, parenthesis, etc. are entirely our creation. One aspect where we are likely to be wrong has to do with the name of people who asked questions and we apologize in advance.

Berkshire Hathaway 2017 Annual Shareholders' Meeting Notes

Saturday, May 06, 2017
CenturyLink Center
455 North 10th Street, Omaha NE 68102

Preliminaries

Opening Multimedia Show

As is the custom of the Berkshire Hathaway Shareholders Meeting, the 2017 session started with a video in which Warren Buffett welcomed the shareholders to the meeting. This is a multimedia extravaganza that precedes the actual meeting.

Berkshire Hathaway shareholders meeting is popularly known as the "Woodstock of Capitalists." So, we know it is not all business. In fact, it is a weekend party of believers in the ideas, values and investment practices of Warren Buffett and Charlie Munger.

The tradition is to kick things off with some entertaining movie prior to the question and answer session.

The preliminary movie is a combination of recap of segments of the history of Berkshire, together with a series of interviews, snippets to showcase either entire Berkshire Hathaway companies (subsidiaries) or individual products, in addition to skits, parodies, cartoons, and real acting by the actual people whose stories are being told to reflect the history and values of the leadership, and in some cases poke fun at personal quirks of leaders of the company. The highlights included events specifically relevant to Berkshire Hathaway in the past year.

The preliminary show also has a serious side to it. One of the well-known values of the leadership of Berkshire is that reputation is everything (addressed many times whenever Warren Buffett or Charlie Munger gets the chance). In that spirit, the preliminaries usually end with Warren Buffett's opening statement before the Subcommittee on Telecommunications and Finance of the Committee on Energy and Commerce of the U.S. House of Representatives in September 1991: "Lose money for the firm and I will be understanding; lose a shred of reputation for the firm and I will be ruthless."

Q&A Format

The format of the 2017 Q&A session followed the standard procedure. Three business journalists—Andrew Ross Sorkin (CNBC and *New York Times*), Becky Quick (CNBC), and Carol Loomis (formerly with *Fortune Magazine*)—chose one-third of the questions. The rest came from shareholders and analysts. Shareholders had e-mailed over two thousand questions to the journalists, who then selected a set of questions most relevant to Berkshire and its operations.

The journalists, who were seated on the stage, alternated with analysts Jay Gelb (Barclays), Jonathan Brandt (Ruane, Cunniff & Goldfarb) and Gregg Warren (Morningstar) and with shareholders in the audience in asking the questions.

Notations

Warren: Warren Buffett, Chairman and CEO of Berkshire Hathaway Inc.
Charlie: Charlie Munger, Vice Chairman of Berkshire Hathaway Inc.
Greg: Greg Abel, Chariman and CEO of Berkshire Hathaway Energy, Vice Chairman of non-insurance operations of Berkshire Hathaway
Jain: Ajit Jain, Vice Chairman of Insurance operations of Berkshire Hathaway
Matt: Matt Rose, Executive Chairman of BNSF
BNSF: Burlington Northern Santa Fe

Preliminary Remarks from Warren Buffett

Warren: Thank you and good morning. That's Charlie, I'm Warren. You can tell us apart, because he can hear and I can see. That's why we work together so well. We each have our specialty. I like to welcome you ... we got lots of out of towners here. I like welcome them to Omaha. [applause] It's a terrific city. Charlie lives in California now for about 70 years but he's still got a lot of Omaha in him. Both of us were born within two miles of this building that you are in. And Charlie, as he mentioned in his description of his amorous triumphs in high school, Charlie graduated from Central High, which is about one mile from here. It's a public school. And my dad, my first wife, my three children and two of my grandchildren all graduated from the same school. In fact, my grandchildren said that they've had the same teachers as my dad. [laughter] It's a great city. I hope you get to see a lot of it while you are here. In just a minute, we will start the question period, hopefully a question and answer period that will last till about noon and then we will take a break for an hour or so. We will reconvene at 1 and then we will continue with the question and answer period till 3:30 and then we'll break for 15 minutes or so. And we will convene the annual meeting of Berkshire. We have three propositions that people wish to speak on. So that could last perhaps as long as an hour.

Before we start, I would like to make a couple of introductions. The first being Carrie Sova, who has been with us for about 7 years. Can we have a light on Carrie? Carrie, are you there? Standup Carrie, come on. [applause]. Carrie puts on this whole program. She came to us about seven years ago and a few years ago, I said, why don't you just put on the annual meeting for me and she handles it all. She has two young children and she has dozens and dozens of exhibitors that she works with and as you can imagine with all of what we put on, with all of the hotels and airlines and rental cars and

18

everything – she does it as if she can do that and be juggling three balls also at the same time. She is amazing and I want to thank her for putting on this program for us. [applause]

Also, I would like to welcome and have you welcome our directors, ... they will be voted on later. I will do that alphabetically. They are in the front row and if you can have the spot light on them as they are introduced and alphabetically - Howard Buffett, Steve Burke, Sue Decker, Bill Gates, Sandy Gottesman, Charlotte Guyman, we have Charlie Munger next to me, Tom Murphy, Ron Olsen, Walter Scott and Meryl Witmer. [applause]. One more introduction I am going to make but I will save that for just a minute.

Our earnings report was put out yesterday. As we regularly explain - the realized investment gains or losses in any period really mean nothing. We could take a lot of gains if we wanted to or we could take a lot of losses if we wanted to but we don't really think about the timing of what we do at all, except in relation to the intrinsic value of what we are buying or selling. We do not make earnings forecasts. On March 31st, we have over $90B of net unrealized gains so if we wanted to report almost any number you can think of and count capital gains as part of the earnings, we can do it. I would say this – that we have a very very slight preference this year, if everything else were equal, (well it's true in any year but a little more so this year) we would rather take losses than gains because of the tax effect, if two securities were equally valued. And there's probably just one touch more emphasis on this this year because we are taxed on gains at 35%, which means we also get the benefit – a tax benefit of 35% of any losses that we take. I would say that there is some chance that rate being lower meaning the losses would have less tax value to us after this year than this year. That is not a big deal but it would be a very slight preference. And it may get to be more of a factor in deferring any gains and perhaps accelerating any losses as the year gets closer to December 31st, assuming (and I am making no predictions about it) ... but assuming that there were to be a tax act that had the effect of reducing earnings.

So, in the first quarter insurance underwriting was the swing factor and there is a lot more about this in our 10-Q which you can look up on the Internet. And if you are seriously interested in evaluating our earnings or our businesses, you should go to the 10-Q because the summary report, as we point out every quarter, doesn't really get to the main points of valuation. I would just mention two factors in conjunction with the insurance situation which I love. In the first four months, not the first three months, the first four month, GEICO had a net gain of some 700,000 policyholders and that's the highest number I can remember. There may have been a figure larger than that somewhere in the past but I didn't go back and look at them all. But last year, I believe the figure was 300,000 and this has been a wonderful period for us at GEICO, because several of our major competitors have decided - and they publicly stated this and, in fact, one of them just reiterated it the other day although they've now changed their policy - but they intentionally cut back on new business because new business carries with it a significant loss in the first year. There is just cost of acquiring new business plus the loss ratio, strangely enough, on first year business tends to run almost 10 points higher than on renewal business. So not only do you have acquisition cost but you actually have higher loss ratio. So, when you run a lot of new businesses, you are going to lose money on that portion of the business that year and we wrote a lot of new business and at least two of our competitors announced that they were lightening up for a while on new business because they did not want to pay the penalty of the first-year loss. And, of course, that opened the door for us and we just put our foot to the floor and try to write as much good business as we can and there are costs to that. A second factor – well it's not a factor in the P&L but an important event in the first quarter – is that we increased our float and on the slide I believe it shows that year over year $16 billion and $14 billion of that came in the first quarter of this year. We had a $14 billion increase in float! For some years I have been telling you that it would be hard to increase the float at all and I still will say the same thing. But it's nice to have $14 billion or more, which is one reason, if you look at our 10-Q, you will see that our cash and cash equivalents including Treasury-bills now comes to well over $90 billion. So I feel very good about the first quarter even though our operating earnings were down a little bit. But one quarter means nothing. I mean, over time, what really counts is whether we are building the value of the businesses that we own and I am always interested in the current figures but I am always dreaming about the future figures.

Introducing Jack Bogle[2]

There is one more person I would like to introduce to you here today and I am quite sure he is here. I haven't seen him but I understood he was coming. I believe that he has made it today. That is Jack Bogle, who I talked about in the annual report. Jack Bogle has probably done more for the American investor than any man in the country. [applause] Jack, would you stand up. [standing ovation]. There he is. Jack Bogle, many years ago… he was not the only one talking about index fund but it wouldn't have happened without him. Paul Samuelson talked about it, Ben Graham even talked about it. The truth is that it was not in the interest of the investment industry, of Wall Street - it was not in their interest to actually have the development of the index fund because it brought down fees dramatically. We've talked about it some in the report and other people commented about it. Index funds,

[2] Founder of The Vanguard Group Inc. and President of Vanguard Bogle Financial Markets Research Center

overall, have delivered for shareholders, a result has been better than Wall Street professionals as a whole and part of the reason for that is they brought down the costs very significantly. So when Jack started, ... very few people ..., certainly Wall Street didn't applaud him and he was the subject to some derision and a lot of attacks. And now we are talking trillions that go into index funds and we are talking a few basis points when we talk about investment fees in the case of index funds, but it is still hundreds of basis points when we talk about fees elsewhere. And I estimate that Jack, at a minimum, has saved - left in the pockets of - investors without hurting them at all in terms of performance, gross performance; he has put tens and tens and tens of billions into their pockets and that number is going to be hundreds and hundreds of billions over time. So its Jack's 88th birthday on Monday. So I would just say Happy Birthday, Jack. Thank you on behalf of American investors. [applause]. And Jack, I've got great news for you. You are going to be 88 on Monday and in only 2 years you'll be eligible for an executive position at Berkshire, so hang in there buddy.

Q&A Session Begins

OK, we've got a panel of expert journalists on this side, expert analysts on that side and expert shareholders in the middle. We are going to rotate – starting with the analysts. Here we go. We will do this through the afternoon. If we get through 54 questions, which would be 6 for each journalist, 6 for each analyst and 18 more for the audience. And then we will go strictly to the audience. I don't think I have got any information as to what the situation is in the overflow room. But we will go to, at least, one of them.

But lets start off with Carol Loomis, of Fortune Magazine, the longest serving employee in the history of Time Inc., I believe for 60 years. Carol, go to it. [applause].

"Ben Franklin, who he [Charlie Munger] worships, said 'an ounce of prevention is worth a pound of cure.' He understated it – an ounce of prevention is worth more than a pound of cure. And I would say a pound of cure promptly applied is worth a ton of cure that's delayed.
Warren Buffett

"I think that a life properly lived is just learn, learn, learn all the time. I think Berkshire has gained enormously from these investment decisions by learning through a long long period."
Charlie Munger

"I have a friend who says 'the first rule of fishing is to fish where the fish are and the second rule of fishing is to never forget the first rule' and we've gotten good at fishing where the fish are."
Charlie Munger

Questions and Answers: Part 1

WELLS FARGO AND IT'S DECENTRALIZED STRUCTURE

Q1. Carol Loomis: Thank you. Thanks from all of us journalists up here. I know that there are many many people out there who have sent us questions that aren't going to get answered and I just want to say that it is very hard to get a question and answered. The one thing that I can suggest is that you follow Warren's thought in the annual report: that he wants everybody to away from this meeting more educated about Berkshire than they were when they came. One way you can do that is to keep your questions quite directly Berkshire related or relating to the annual letter. Even then it would be hard to get your questions answered. The three of us have only 18 questions in total. But I encourage you to think in the Berkshire related direction when you are submitting your question next year.

Now my first question is about Wells Fargo, which is Berkshire's largest equity holding, $28 billion at the end of the year. This question comes from a shareholder who did not wish to be identified. In the wake of the sales practices scandal that last year engulfed the Wells Fargo, the company's independent directors commissioned an investigation and hired a large law firm to assist in carrying it out. The findings of the investigation, which were harsh, have been released in what is called the Wells Fargo Sales Practices Report, which can be found on the internet. It concludes that a major part of the company's problem was that "Wells Fargo's decentralized corporate structure gave too much autonomy to the community banks' senior leadership."

Mr. Buffett, how do you satisfy yourself that Berkshire

isn't subject to the same risk, with its highly-decentralized structure and the very substantial autonomy given to senior leadership of the operating companies?

Warren: Yah, it's true that we at Berkshire probably operate – we certainly operate on a more decentralized plan than any company remotely our size and we count very heavily on principles of behavior rather than loads of rules. It's one reason that every annual meeting you see that Salomon description and that's why I write very few communiques to our managers – but I send them one, once every 2 years. It basically says that we've got all the money we need – we would like to have more but it's not a necessity. But we don't have one ounce of reputation more than we need and that our reputation at Berkshire is in their hands. And Charlie and I believe that if you establish the right sort of culture and that culture to some extent self-selects who you obtained as directors and as managers that you will get better results that way in terms of behavior than if you have a thousand-page guidebook. You're going to have problems regardless. We have 367,000, I believe, employees. Now if you have a town of 367,000 households, which is about the Omaha Metropolitan areas, people are doing something wrong as we are talking here today. There is no question about it. The real question is whether the managers are worrying and thinking about finding and correcting any bad behavior and if they fail in that whether the message gets to Omaha and whether we do something about it.

At Wells Fargo, you know there were three very significant mistakes, but there was one that dwarfs all of the others. You are going to have incentive systems in almost any business. There is nothing wrong with incentive systems but you've got to be very careful what you incentivize. And you can't incentivize bad behavior and if so, you better have a system for recognizing it. Clearly, at Wells Fargo, there was an incentive system built around the idea of cross-selling and the number of services per customer. And the company, at every quarterly investor presentation, highlighted how many services per customer. So, that was the focus of the organization, a major focus. And undoubtedly, people got paid, graded and promoted based on that number or at least partly based on that number. Well, it turned out that was incentivizing the wrong kind of behavior. We have made similar mistakes. Any company is going to make a some mistake in designing a system; but it's a mistake and you are going to find out about it at some point. I will get to how we find out about it. But the biggest mistake was that (and I don't obviously know the facts as to how this information got passed up the line at Wells Fargo) …. but at some point, if there is a major problem, the CEO will get wind of it and that is, at that moment, that's the key to everything because the CEO has to act.

That Salomon situation that you saw happened because on April, I think 28th, the CEO of Salomon, the president of Salomon, the general counsel of Salomon sat in a room and they had described to them by a fellow named John Meriwether some bad practice, terrible practice that was being conducted by a fellow named Paul Mozer, who worked for him. And Paul Mozer was flimflamming the U.S. Treasury, which is a very dumb thing to do. And he was doing it partly out of spite because he didn't like the Treasury and they didn't like him. So, he put in phony bids for U.S. Treasuries and all of that. So, on April 28th, roughly, the CEO and all these people knew that they had something that had gone very wrong and they had to report it to the Federal Reserve Bank in New York. The CEO, John Gutfreund, said he would do it and then he didn't do it. He undoubtedly put it off just because it was an unpleasant thing to do, and then on May 15, another Treasury auction was held and Paul Mozer put in a bunch of phony bids again. And at this point it's all over because the top management had known ahead of time and now a guy who is pyromaniac had gone out and lit another fire; and he lit it after they have been warned that he is a pyromaniac, essentially. And it all went downhill from there. It had to stop when the CEO learns about it. Then they made a third mistake actually and but again it pales in comparison to the second mistake.

They made a third mistake when they totally underestimated the impact of what they had done once it became uncovered because there was a penalty of $185 million and in the banking business, people get fined billions and billions of dollars for mortgage practices and all kinds of things. The total fines against the big banks totaled $30 or $40 billion or whatever the number may be. So, they measured the seriousness of the problem by the dimension of the fine and they thought $185 million fine signaled a less offensive practice than something that involved $2 billion and they are totally wrong on that. But the main problem was they didn't act when they learned about it. It's bad enough having a bad system but they didn't act. At Berkshire, the main source of information for me about anything that's being done wrong, at a subsidiary is the hotline – we've got about 4,000 or so hot line reports or communication on the hotlines, perhaps 4,000 times a year. And most of them are frivolous. You know, "the guy next to me has bad breath" or something like that. But there are a few serious ones. And the head of our internal audit, Becki Amick, looks at all those. People, a lot of them coming anonymous, probably most of them and some of them she refers back to the companies, probably most of them. But anything that looks serious, I will hear about and that has led to action - more than once and we spent real money investigating some of those. We put special investigators sometimes on them and, like I said, it has uncovered certain practices that we would not at all condone at the parent company. I think it's a good system but I don't think it's perfect.

I'm sure they've got an internal audit at Wells Fargo. I am sure they got a hotline. I don't know the facts but I would just have to bet that a lot of communications came in on that. I don't know what their system was for getting to the right person and I don't know who did what at any given time. But that would be a huge, huge, huge error if they were getting some communications and they ignored them or they just sent them back down to somebody down below.

Charlie, you followed. What are your thoughts on it?

Charlie: Put me down as skeptical when some law firm thinks they know how to fix something like this. If you're in a business where you have a whole lot of people under incentives that are very likely will create a lot of misbehaviors, of course, you'll need a huge compliance department. Every big warehouse, stock brokerage firm has a huge compliance department. If we had one, we will have a big compliance department too. Wouldn't we, Warren?

Warren: Absolutely.

Charlie: Absolutely, but that doesn't mean that everybody should solve their problems with more and more compliance. I think we've had less troubles over the years by being more careful on whom we picked to have power and having a culture of trust. I think we have less trouble, not more.

Warren: But we will have troubles from time to time.

Charlie: Yes, of course. We will be blind sighted someday.

Warren: Charlie said when Ben Franklin, who he worships, said "an ounce of prevention is worth a pound of cure," he understated it – "an ounce of prevention is worth more than a pound of cure." And I would say a pound of cure promptly applied is worth a ton of cure that's delayed. Problems don't go away. John Gutfruend said that problem originally was, he called it, a traffic ticket. He told the truth there. Salomon was a traffic ticket and it almost brought down a business. Some other CEO described the problem that he encountered as a foot fault and it resulted in an incredible damage to the institution. You've got to act promptly. And frankly, I don't know any better system than hotlines and anonymous letters to me. I get anonymous letters and I got three or four of them probably in the last six or seven years that have resulted in major changes and very very occasionally there are signed but usually almost always they were anonymous. It won't make any diference. There would be no retribution against anybody, obviously, if they call our attention to something that's going wrong. But I will tell you, as we sit here, somebody is doing, quite a few people, are probably doing something wrong at Berkshire. Usually, it is very limited, I mean, maybe stealing small amounts of money or something like that. But when it gets to some sales practice like what is taking place at Wells Fargo, you can see the kind of damage it would do.

We will now shift over the analysts. And Johnny Brandt.

DRIVERLESS CARS AND ITS IMPACT ON GEICO AND BNSF

Q2. Analyst, Jonathan Brandt: Hi Warren, Hi Charlie. Thanks for having me. You addressed the risk of driverless cars to GEICO's business, but it strikes me that driverless trucks could narrow the cost advantage of railroads, even if the number of crewmembers in a locomotive eventually declines from two to zero. Is autonomous technology more of an opportunity or more of a threat for the Burlington Northern?

Warren: I would say that driverless trucks are a lot more of a threat than an opportunity to Burlington Northern. I would say that if driverless cars became pervasive, it would only be because they're safer and that would mean that the overall economic cost of the auto related losses had gone down and that would drive down the premium income of GEICO. So, I would say that autonomous vehicles, widespread, would hurt us if they spread to trucks and they would hurt our auto insurance business. I think, my personal view is they will certainly come. I think they may be a long way off, but that will depend on experience in the first early months of the introduction, in other than test situations. If they make the world safer, it's going to be a very good thing, but it won't be a good thing for auto insurers and, similarly, if they learn how to move trucks more safely (there tends to be driver shortages in the truck business now) it obviously improves their position vis-a-vis the railroads.

Charlie?

Charlie: Well, I think that's perfectly clear. [laughter]

Warren: Finally, approval, all these years. [laughter]

OK. Station 1, shareholder.

HITTING THE SWEET SPOTS IN INVESTING

Q3. Audience, Station 1: Hi Warren and Charlie, I am Brian Martin. I am from Springfield, Illinois. In HBO documentary, *Becoming Warren Buffett,* you had a great analogy comparing investing to hitting a baseball and knowing your sweet spot. Ted Williams knew his sweet spot was a pitch right down the middle. When both of you look at potential investments, what attributes make a company, a pitch in your sweet spot that you'll take a swing at and invest in?

Warren: Well, I am not sure I'll define it in exactly the terms you would like. But the way we sort of know it when we see it is that it would tend to be a business that, for one reason or another, we can look out 5 or 10 or 20 years and decide that the competitive advantage that it had, at the present, would last over that period and it would have a trusted manager that would not only fit into the Berkshire culture, but that was eager to join the Berkshire culture. Then it would be a matter of price. But the main thing when we buy a business is essentially that we are laying out a lot of money now, based on what we think that business will deliver over time. The higher the certainty with which we make that prediction, the better we feel about it. We can go back to the first – it was not the first outstanding business we bought – but it was kind of a watershed event, which was a relatively small company, See's Candy. The question when we looked at See's Candy in 1972 was – would people still want to be both eating and giving away that candy in preference to other candies and it wouldn't be a question of people buying candy for the low bid and we had a manager we liked very much. Then we bought the business for which we paid $25 million net of cash and it was earning about $4 million pretax then and we must be getting close to $2 billion or something like that pretax that we've taken out of it. It was only because we felt that people would not be buying necessarily a lower priced candy. I mean, it does not work very well. If you go to your wife or your girlfriend on Valentine's Day (I hope they're the same person) [laughter] and say "here's a box of candy honey, I took the low bid." It loses a little … as you go through that speech. So, we made a judgement about See's Candy that it would be special, probably not in the year 2017, but we certainly thought it would be special in 1982 and 1992 and fortunately, we were right on it. We are looking for more See's Candy, only a lot bigger.

Charlie?

Charlie: It's also true that we were young and ignorant then.

Warren: Now we're old and ignorant. [laughter]

Charlie: Yes, that's true too. And the truth of the matter is we would have been very wise to buy See's Candy at a slightly higher price. And if he had asked for it, we wouldn't have done it. So, we've gotten a lot of credit for being smarter than we were.

Warren: Yah, to be more accurate, if it had been been $5 million more, I wouldn't have bought it. Charlie would have been willing to buy it. Fortunately, we didn't have to go to the point where we had to make the decision that way. But he would have pushed forward when I probably would have faded. It's a good thing that the guy came around. Actually, the seller was the grandson of Mrs. See, wasn't he Charlie? or Larry See's son? Am I correct? Or Larry See's brother. But he was not interested in the business and he was more interested in girls and graves actually. He almost changed his mind. He did change his mind about selling. And I was not there. But Rick Guerin told me that Charlie went and gave an hour talk on the merits of girls and graves over having a candy company. [laughter] This is true folks. And the fellow sold to us. I pull Charlie out in emergencies like that.

Charlie: We were very lucky that, early, the habit of buying horrible business because they were really cheap gave us a lot of experience trying to fix unfixable businesses as they headed downward toward doom. And that early experience was so horrible - fixing the unfixable - that we were good at avoiding them thereafter. So, I would argue that our early stupidity helped us.

Warren: Yah. We learned that we could not make a silk purse out of a sow's ear.

Charlie: We learned it.

Warren: We went on looking for silk after that.

Charlie: You had to try hard for a long time, to fail and to have your nose rubbed in it, to really understand it.

Warren: Okay, Becky Quick.

REVISION OF BERKSHIRE STOCK HOLDINGS

Q4. Journalist, Becky Quick: This question comes from a shareholder named Mark Blackley, Tulsa, Oklahoma. He said, "there has been more news than usual in some of Berkshire's core stock holdings, Wells Fargo and the incentive and new account scandals, American Express losing the Costco relationship and playing catch up in the premium card space. United Airlines in customer service issues, Coca-Cola and slowing soda consumption. How much time is spent reviewing Berkshire's stock holdings and is it safe to assume if Berkshire continues to hold these stocks that the thesis remains intact?"

Warren: We spend a lot of time thinking. Those are very large holdings. If you add up American Express and Coca-Cola and Wells Fargo, you're getting up well into the high tens of billions of dollars and those are businesses we like very much but they have different characteristics. In the case of (you mentioned United Airlines), we actually are the largest holder of the four largest airlines and that is much more of an industry thought. But all businesses have problems and some of them have some very big pluses. You mentioned American Express, if you read American Express's first quarter report and talk about their Platinum card, it's doing very well. The gains around the world, I think there were 17% or something like that on buildings in the UK and 15% in the original currency or the local currency in Japan, Mexico and very good in the United States. There is competition in all of these businesses. We did not buy American Express or Wells Fargo or United Airlines, or Coca Cola with the idea that they would never have problems or never have competition. Why we did buy them was we thought they had very strong hands and we liked the financial policies and in case of many of them, we like their position.

We bought a lot of businesses and we do look to see where we think they have durable competitive advantage and we recognize, that if you have a very good business, you're going to have plenty of competitors that are going to try and take it away from you and then you make a judgement as to the ability of your particular company and product and management to ward off competitors. They won't go away but we think (and I am not going to get into specific names on that) those companies are generally very well positioned and I have likened them, essentially. If you get wonderful business, even if it's a small company like See's Candy, you basically have an economic castle. In capitalism, people are going to try and take that castle away from you. So, you want a moat around it, protecting it in various ways that it can be protected and then you want a knight in the castle who is pretty darn good at warding off marauders. But there are going to be marauders and they will never go away.

I think Coca-Cola [was started] in 1886 and American Express was in, I don't know 1851 or 1852, starting out with an express business. Wells Fargo, I don't know what year they started. Incidentally, American Express was started by Wells and Fargo as well. These companies had lots of challenges and they will have more challenges and the companies we owned have had challenges. Our insurance businesses have had challenges, but you know, we started with National Indemnity, $8 million purchase in 1968, and fortunately, we've had people like Tony Nicely at GEICO and Ajit Jain who have added tens of billions of value. We've got some smaller companies that you probably don't even know about but have really done terrific job for us. So there will always be competition in insurance, but there will always be things to do that are really intelligent management, with a decent distribution system, various things going for them, to ward off marauders. So, the specific question how much time is spent reviewing the holdings, I would say I do it every day and I'm sure Charlie does it every day.

Charlie: I don't think I have anything to add to that either. [laughter]

Warren: We will cut his salary if he doesn't participate. [laughter]

Okay, Jay Gelb.

REINSURANCE DEAL WITH AIG

Q5. Analyst, Jay Gelb: This question is on Berkshire's retroactive reinsurance deal with AIG, which was the largest ever of its kind. Based on AIG's track record of reserve deficiencies and the opportunity for Berkshire to invest the float, what is your level of confidence that this contract covering up to $20 billion of AIG's reserves, in return for $10 billion of premiums, will ultimately be profitable for Berkshire?

Warren: Well, at the time we do every deal, I think it's smart and sometimes I find out otherwise as we go along. The deal (that Jay knows but might be unfamiliar to many people) is that AIG transferred to us the liability for 80% of $25 bilion in excess of $25 billion. In other words, they had to pay the first $25 billion and then on the next $25 billion we had to pay 80% of what they paid, up to a limit of $20 billion, that is 80% of $25 billion. And we got paid $10.2 billion for that. This applies with their losses in many classes of business written or earned before December 31, 2015. So Ajit Jain – who has made a lot more for Berkshire, for you, than I have (but he evaluates that sort of transaction). And we talk about it a fair amount ourselves. I just find it interesting. I particularly find the $10.2 billion that they are going to give us interesting. And we've come to the conclusion that we think we'll do well by getting $10.2 billion today with a maximum payout of $20 billion over some indefinite period of time – between now and judgement day – on this large piece of business. AIG had very good reasons for doing this because their reserves had been under criticism and essentially it should have put to bed the question whether or not they were under-reserved on that business. We get the $10.2 billion and the question is how fast we pay out the money and how much money we pay out. Ajit does 99% of the thinking on that and I do 1% and we project out what we think will happen, and we know that whatever our projection is, it will be wrong, but we try to be conservative.

We've done a fair amount of these deals. This is the largest. The second largest was a creature that was formed out of Lloyds of London some years ago. We've been wrong on one transaction that involved something over a billion of premium – I mean, clearly we were wrong. And there are a couple of others that may or may not work out depending on what you assume we have earned on the funds. But they are ok, but they probably didn't come out as well as we thought they would though. But overall, we have done ok on this. It's less ok when we are sitting around with $90 plus billion of cash, so the incremental $10.2 billion we took in, in the first quarter, is earning us peanuts at the moment and peanuts is not what fits into the formula for making us an attractive deal. So, we do have to assume we will find uses of the money. But the money will be with us for quite a while and I think our calculations are on the conservative side. They are not the identical calculations that AIG makes; we come up with our own estimates of payouts in all of that. Actually, I think it was quite a good transaction from AIG's stand point, because they did take $20 billion of potential losses off of the $10.2 billion and I think they satisfied the investing community that they were quite unlikely to have adverse development in the period prior to 2015 that was not accounted for by this transaction.

Charlie?

Charlie: Well, I think it's intrinsically a dangerous kind of activity, but that is one of its attractions. I don't think there are any two people in the world that are better at this kind of transaction than Ajit and Warren and nobody else has had the experience we've had. Just get me in a lot more of these businesses and I'll accept a little extra worry.

Warren: There is one thing that I should mention here. We actually were the only insurance operation in the world that would write that sort of a contract where it would be satisfactory to the other party. When somebody hands you $10.2 billion and says I'm counting on you to pay $20 billion back, even if it's 50 years from now on the last dollar, there are very few people they want to hand $10.2 billion to. There is limited people on the other side that can remotely have that size of deal.

Charlie: Very few is a good expression; he means one. [laughter]

Warren: OK, we will go to Station 2.

CHARLIE MUNGER'S FAVORITE NEGOTIATION

Q6. Audience, Station 2: Hello Mr. Buffett, Mr. Munger. My name is Grant Gibson. I am from Denver, Colorado and this is my fifth consecutive year here. So, thank you

for having us.

Warren: Thanks for coming.

Grant Gibson: I appreciate it. With all due respect, Mr. Buffett, this question is for Mr. Munger. In your career of thousands of negotiations in business dealings, could you describe for the crowd, which one sticks out in your mind as your favorite or as otherwise noteworthy?

Charlie: Oh, I don't think I have got a favorite, but the one that probably did us the most good as a learning experience was See's Candy. It's just the power of the brand and the unending flow of ever-increasing money with no work. [laughter]

Grant: Sounds nice.

Charlie: I'm not sure if we would have bought Coca-Cola if we he hadn't bought the See's. I think that a life properly lived is just learn, learn, learn all the time. I think Berkshire gained enormously from these investment decisions by learning through a long long period. Every time you appoint a new person that's never had big capital allocation experience, it's like rolling the dice. We are way better where we have done it so long and the decisions blend and the one feature that comes through, is the continuous learning. If we had not kept learning, you wouldn't even be here. You'd be alive, probably, but not here. [laughter].

Warren: There's nothing like the pain of being in a lousy business. It makes you appreciate a good one.

Charlie: Well, I don't think I'm getting into a really good one. That's a very personal experience and it's a learning experience. I have a friend who says – "the first rule of fishing is to fish where the fish are and the second rule of fishing is to never forget the first rule" and we've gotten good at fishing where the fish are.

Warren: That's only metaphorically. I went to fish with Charlie one time.

Charlie: There's too many other boats in the damn water. But the fish are still there.

Warren: We bought a department store in Baltimore in 1966 and there's really nothing like being in an experience in trying to decide whether you're going to put a new store in an area that hasn't really developed yet enough to support it, but your competitor may move there first and then you have the decision on whether to jump in and if you jump in, that kind of spoils it, now you got two stores, where even one store isn't quite justified. How to play those games – those business games, you learn a lot by trying and what you really learn is which ones to avoid. If you just stay out of a bunch of terrible businesses; you're off to a very great start, because we've tried them all.

Charlie: You can really learn a lot because the experience is like eating a lot of cockle burgers and it really gets your attention.

Warren: Well, we won't expand on that. [laughter] Andrew Ross Sorkin.

INVESTING IN TECHNOLOGY COMPANIES

Q7. Journalist, Andrew Ross Sorkin: Good morning, Warren. This question comes from a long-time shareholder, who I should tell you accosted me last night in the lobby of the Hilton Hotel with this question. Warren, for years you stayed away from technology companies saying they were too hard to predict and

didn't have moats. Then you seemed to change your view about technology when you invested in IBM and again when you recently invested in Apple, but then on Friday you said IBM had not met your expectations and sold a third of our stake. Do you view IBM and Apple differently and what have you learned about investing in technology companies?

Warren: Well, I do view them differently. But obviously, when I bought the IBM, started buying it six years ago, I thought it would do better in the six years that have elapsed than it has. Apple, I regard them as being quite different businesses. I think Apple is much more of a consumer products business in terms of sort of analyzing moats around it in consumer behavior and all that sort of things. So, obviously, a product with all kinds of tech built into it, but in terms of laying out what their prospective customers will do in the future as opposed to, say, IBM's customers, it's a different sort of analysis. But that doesn't mean it's correct and we will find out over time. But, they are two different types of decisions and I was wrong on the first one and we'll find out whether I'm right or wrong on the second. I don't regard them as apples and apples and I don't quire regard them as apples and oranges, but it's somewhat in between on that.

Charlie?

Charlie: Well, we avoided the tech stocks because we felt we had no advantage there and other people did. And I think that's a good idea not to play where the other people who are better. But you know if you ask me in retrospect, what was our worst mistake in the tech field. I think we were smart enough to figure out Google; those ads work so much better in the early days than anything else, so I would say that we failed you there. We were smart enough to do it but didn't do it and we do that all the time too.

Warren: We were their customer very early on with GEICO, for example; and these figures are way out of date as I remember, we were paying them $10 or $11 a click, or something like that. And anytime you're paying someone $10 or $11 every time somebody just punches a little thing where you have no cost at all, that's a good business unless someone is going to take it away from you. So, we were close up seeing the impact of that. (And incidentally, if any of you don't have anything to do at your hotel room tonight, just keep punching Progressive or something. [laughter]. Don't really do that. The thought just happened to cross my mind.) We've almost never seen a business like that, and I think for Lasik surgery and things like that, I think the figures were $60 or $70 a click, with no incremental costs.

I knew the guys, they actually designed their prospectus and they came to see me. And a little bit after the original one they went public. I had plenty of ways to ask questions or anything of that sort to educate myself. But I blew it.

Charlie: We blew Walmart too. It was a total cinch. We were smart enough to figure that out, but we didn't.

Warren: Figuring out … execution is what really counts. I could be making two mistakes on IBM. It's harder to predict, in my view, the winners in various items, or how much price competition will enter into something like cloud services and all that.

I made a statement the other day. It's really remarkable (and I asked Charlie if he could think of a situation like it), where one person has built an extraordinary economic machine in two really pretty different industries almost simultaneously, as has happened …

Charlie: from a standing start of zero

Warren: … from a standing start of zero, with competitors with lots of capital and everything else, to do it in retailing and to do it with the cloud, like Jeff Bezos has done. People like the Mellons invested in lot of different industries and all of that but he (Bezos) has been, in effect, the CEO simultaneously, of two businesses starting from scratch. Andy Grove from Intel used to say, "think about if you had a silver bullet and could shoot it and get rid of one of your competitors, who would it be?" Well, I think both in the cloud and in retail, there are a lot of people that would aim that silver bullet at Jeff. It's a different sort of game. You know, with The Washington Post, that he played that hand as well as anybody possibly could. It's a remarkable business achievement where he has been involved, actually, in the execution, not just bankrolling it, of two businesses that are probably as feared by their competitors almost, as any you can find.

Charlie? Any further thoughts?

Charlie: We are sort of like the Mellons – old fashioned people who've done all right and Jeff Bezos is a different species.

Warren: And we missed it entirely, incidentally. We never owned a share of Amazon.

OK, Gregg Warren.

INVESTING IN MAJOR AIRLINES

Q8. Analyst, Gregg Warren: Warren, my question relates to some recent stock purchases as well. Unlike the railroads which benefits from colossal barriers to entry, due to their established, practically impossible to replicate networks of rail and rights of way, the airline industry seems to have few, if any, advantages. Even with the consolidation we've seen during the past 15

years, the barriers to entry are few and the exit barriers are high. The industry also suffers from low switching costs and intense pricing competition and is heavily exposed to fuel cost, with rising fuel prices being difficult to pass on and declining fuel prices leading to more price competition. Compare this with real customers who have few choices and thus with limited buying power and where fuel charges allow the industry to mitigate fuel price fluctuations. While you've noted several times since the series of airline purchases were announced, that the two industries are quite different, and that comparisons should not be made to Berkshire's move into railroads a decade ago, could you walk us through what convinced you that the airlines were different enough this time around for Berkshire to invest close to $10 billion in the four major airlines? Because it would seem to me that UPS, which you have a small stake in and FedEx, both of which have wider economic moats built on more identifiable and durable competitive advantages, would be a better option for long-term investors.

Warren: The decision in respect to airlines had no connection with our being involved in the railroad business. I mean, you can classify them as maybe as transportation businesses or something; but it had no more connection than the fact we owned GEICO or any other business.

You couldn't have picked a tougher industry ever since Orville went up. And I've said if anybody really had been thinking about investors, they should have had Wilbur shoot him down and save everyone a lot of money for 100 years. You can go to the Internet and type in "airlines and bankrupt", and you'll see something like 100 airlines, in that general range, that have gone bankrupt in the last few decades. Actually, Charlie and I were directors for some time of US Air and people write about how terrible an experience thye've had in US Air. It was one of the dumbness things I've ever done

Charlie: And we made a lot of money out of it too.

Warren: Yeah, we made a lot of money out of it because there was one little brief period when people got all enthused about US Air. And after we left as directors and after we sold our position, US Air managed to go bankrupt twice in the subsequent period.

I mean you've named - not all of them - but a number of factors that just make for terrible economics. I will tell you that it's a fiercely competitive industry. The question is, whether it's a suicidally competitive industry, which it used to be. When you get virtually every one of the major carriers and dozens and dozens and dozens of minor carriers going bankrupt, it ought to come to a point where you realize maybe you are in the wrong industry.

It has been operating for some time now at 80% or better of capacity, being available seat miles and you can see what deliveries are going to be and that sort of thing. I think it's fair to say that they will operate at higher degrees of capacity over the next 5 or 10 years than the historical rates, which caused all of them to go broke. Now the question is whether even when they are doing it in the 80's, they will do suicidal things in terms of pricing remains to be seen.

They actually, at present, are earning quite high returns on invested capital, I think higher than either FedEx or UPS if you actually check that out. But that doesn't mean tomorrow morning, you know if you're running one of those airlines and if the other guy cuts his prices, you cut your prices and as you say, there's more flexibility when fuel goes down to bring down prices, than there is to raise prices when prices go up. It is no cinch that the industry will have some more pricing sensibility in the next 10 years, than they had in the last 100 years. But the conditions have improved for that. They've got more labor stability than they had before, because basically they've all been through bankruptcy and they're all going to sort of have an industry pattern bargaining. It looks to me like they're going to have a shortage of pilots to some degree, but it's not like buying See's Candy.

Charlie?

Charlie: No, but the investment world has gotten tougher with more competition and more affluence and more absolute obsession with finance throughout the whole country. We picked up a lot of low hanging fruit in the old days, where it was very, very easy and where we had huge margins of safety. Now we operate with a less advantageous general climate and maybe we have small statistical advantages, where in the old days it was like shooting fish in a barrel. But that's all right. Its ok when it gets a little harder after you get filthy rich.

Warren: Charlie is more philosophical than I am on that point.

Charlie: I can't bring back the low hanging fruits, Warren. You just have to keep reaching for the higher branches.

Warren: Gregg, I think the odds are very high, that there are more revenue passenger miles, five years from now or ten years from now. If the airline companies are only worth, five or ten years from now, what they are worth now in terms of equity, we'll get a pretty reasonable rate of return because they are going to buy back a lot of stock at fairly low multiples. So, if the company is worth the same amount at the end of the year and there are fewer shares of stock outstanding, overtime, we make decent money and all four of the major airlines are buying their stocks...

Charlie: You've got to remember that the railroads were a terrible business for decades and decades and decades, and then they got good.

Warren: I like the position. Obviously, by buying all four, it means that it is very hard to distinguish, at least in my mind, who will do the best. I think the odds are quite high, that if you take revenue passenger miles, flown five or ten years from now, it will be a higher number. There will be low cost people who'll come in and, you know, the Spirits of the world or JetBlues, and whatever may be. My guess is that all four of the companies that we have will have higher revenues. The question is what their operating ratio is. They will have fewer shares outstanding by a significant margin, so, even if they are worth what they are worth today, we could make a fair amount of money, but it is no cinch playing a long shot.

OK, Station 3.

BERKSHIRE'S INVESTMENT IN COCA-COLA

Q9. Audience, Station 3: Good morning, everybody. My name is Sibylle Arians. I am from Germany and I am a member of Board of Ethecon Foundation, Ethics and Economy. I am very happy that I put my question here and may be you are not as happy as I am to listen to it.

Warren: Well, we will try to stay happy. Thank you for coming.

Sibylle: Thank you. Mr. Buffett, a few years ago I saw a movie in which you proclaimed that the print out on the dollar bill "In God we Trust" does not really express your philosophy. In your opinion only cash counts and your credo is "In the Dollar I Trust."

Warren: I don't think I've ever said that actually.

Sibylle: Well, I can send you the movie that will prove.

Warren: Send me a clip of the movie.

Sibylle: Maybe you were just joking, but always behind a joke, there is also a truth. You laughed heartily at that moment. You, as one of the most richest men of all times on this earth, a good-humored friendly elderly gentleman. Whatever motivated those who designed the dollar notes, they certainly wanted to say that there is something higher than the value of this printed paper. Regrettably, you have shown many times in your life that you see this differently.

You have accumulated billions of dollars, showed extraordinary cleverness and skill and you know better to pick up than many others who, like you, use the rules which are inherent to capitalism for their own intentions. But have you ever given a thought to what troubles and sacrifices, slavery and destruction of mother earth and even diseases and deaths, stick to the dollar bills, which you gather so eagerly? Let's take Coca-Cola. Ethecon Foundation, Ethics and Economy from Germany has awarded the Black Planet Award to all the members of the board of directors, as well as to the large shareholders, Warren Buffett and Herbert Allen because you are co-responsible for all of what makes these groups make so much money, isn't it? Among other things, Coca-Cola deprives people of their drinking water in draught prone areas of the world and many destruct and contaminate the ground water in these areas.

Warren: I don't want to interrupt you, but are you making a speech or asking a question?

Sibylle: I will put my question right now.

Warren: Ok, good.

Sibylle: Will you give up your Coca-Cola shares if the

destruction of the environment, the monopolization of the right to healthy drinking water, and the shameless exploitation of the workers continue?

Charlie: Well that's more of a speech than a question. [applause].

Warren: I don't think that quote that you had earlier, I've said once or twice, it should say "In the Federal Reserve We Trust," because they print the money and if they print too much of it, it could decline in value but, to my knowledge, I have never said anything like you originally said and I would say this – I've been eating things I like to eat all my life. This Coca-Cola is 12 oz., I drink about five a day, it has about 1.2 oz. of sugar in it and if you look at what different people get their sugar and calories from, they get them from all kinds of things. I happen to believe that I like to get 1.2 oz. with this and it's enjoyable.

Since 1886 people have found it pleasant and I would say that, if you pick every meal in terms of what somebody in some recent publications told you that it's the very best for you, I'd offer you that and say go to it. But if you told me that I would live one year longer, if I'd eat nothing but broccoli and asparagus and everything my aunt Alice wanted me to eat all my life, or I would eat everything I enjoyed eating, including chocolate sundaes and Coca-Cola, steak and hash browns, I would rather eat in a way I enjoy for my whole life, [laughter] than eat some other way and live another year.

I do think that choice should be mine. If somebody decides sugar is harmful, maybe it will encourage the government to ban sugar, but sugar in Coca-Cola is not different than eating sugar put on my grape nuts in the morning or whatever else I'm having. So, I think Coca-Cola has been a very very positive factor in America and the world for a long long time and you can look at a list of achievements of the company [laughter] and I really don't want anyone telling me I can't drink it.

Charlie: Well, I've solved my Coca-Cola problem by drinking Diet Coke, and I swill the stuff like other people swill I don't know what. I've been doing it for just as long as you have been taking those Coca-Colas for. I've had breakfast before with Warren, when he has Coca-Colas and nuts.

Warren: It's pretty damn good too.

Charlie: If you keep doing it, Warren, you may not make a hundred.

Warren: I think there's something in longevity about feeling happy about your life too.

Charlie: Absolutely. [applause].

Warren: OK, Carol.

BERKSHIRE'S INTRINSIC VALUE

Q10. Journalist, Carol Loomis: This question is from France Tromburger of Austria and it concerns intrinsic value, which is neither, (Warren may amend this my definition here) but which is neither a company's accounting value nor it's stock market value, but is rather its estimated real value. So, the question is: at what rate has Berkshire compounded intrinsic value over the last 10 years and at what rate, including your explanation for it please, do you think intrinsic value can be compounded over the next 10 years?

Warren: Intrinsic value can only be calculated, or gains, in retrospect, but the intrinsic value pure definition would be the cash to be generated between now and judgment day discounted at an interest rate that seems appropriate at the time, and that has varied enormously over a 30 or 40 year period. If you pick out 10 years and you are back to May of

2007, we had some unpleasant things coming up but, I would say, that we've probably compounded a t about 10% and I think that is going to be tough to achieve; in fact, almost impossible to achieve, if we continued in this interest rate environment.

If you asked me to give the answer to the question, if I could only pick one statistic to ask you about the future, before I gave the answer, I would not ask you about GDP growth, I would not ask you about who was going to be President. I would ask you what the interest rate would be over the next 20 years on average, the 10 year or whatever you wanted to do. If you assume our present interest rate structure is likely to be the average over 10 or 20 years, then I would say it would be very difficult to get the 10 percent. On the other hand, if I were to pick, with a whole range of probabilities on interest rates, I would say that, that rate might be, it might be somewhat aspirational and it might be doable. You would say, well we can't continue these interest rates for a long time. But I would ask you to look at Japan, where 25 years ago, we couldn't see how their interest rates could be sustained and we're still looking at the same thing. So, I do not think it's easy to predict the course of interest rates at all and, unfortunately, predicting that is embedded in giving a good answer to you. I would say the chances of getting a terrible result in Berkshire, are probably as low as about anything you can find. The chances of getting a sensational result are also about as low as anything you can find. My best guess would be in the 10% range, but that assumes somewhat higher interest rates, not dramatically higher, but somewhat higher interest rates in the next 10 or 20 years than we've experienced in the last 7 years.

Charlie: Well, there's no question about the fact that the future, with our present size is, in terms of percentage rates of return is going to be less glorious than our past. We keep saying that and now we're proving it. [laughter].

Warren: You want to end on that note, Charlie, or would you care?

Charlie: Well, I do think Warren is right about one thing. I think we have a collection of businesses that on average, has better investment values than say the S&P average. So, I don't think you shareholders have a terrible terrible problem.

Warren: I would say we probably, I think we are certain, that we do have more of a shareholder orientation than the S&P 500 as a whole. I mean, this company has a culture where decisions are made as an owner, as a private owner would make them. Frankly, that's a luxury we have that many companies don't have. I mean they are under pressures today, sometimes to do things. One of the questions I ask the CEO of every public company that I meet is, what would you be doing differently if you owned it all yourself? The answer, you know, is usually this, that and a couple of other things. If you would ask us, the answer is we will be doing exactly what we are doing, if we owned all the stock ourselves and I think that is a small plus over time. Anything further, Charlie? [applause].

Charlie: I think we have one other advantage - a lot of other people are trying to be brilliant and we are just trying to stay rational. [applause]. And it's a big advantage. Ttrying to be brilliant is very dangerous, particularly when you're gambling.

Warren: OK, Jonathan.

"I had an aunt Katy here in Omaha, Charlie knew well, who worked for her husband, as did I and she worked hard all her life and had lived in a house she paid $8,000 for, 45th and Hickory all her life. Because she was in Berkshire (she lived until she was 97), she ended up with a few hundred million. She would write me a letter every four or five months and would say, "Dear Warren, I hate to bother you, but am I going to run out of money?" I would write her back and say, "Dear Katy, it's a good question because if you lived 986 years, you're going to run out of money." About four or five months later, she would write me the same letter again."
Warren Buffett

"I don't think we'd be having these big shareholder meetings if there weren't a little bit of teaching ethos in Berkshire and I have watched it closely for a long time. I'd argue that, that's what we are trying to do: to set a proper example, stay sane, and be honest."
Charlie Munger

BERKSHIRE'S DEFERRED TAX LIABILITY

Q11. Analyst, Jonathan Brandt: If corporate tax rates are reduced meaningfully, Berkshire will enjoy a onetime boost to book value, because of its sizable deferred tax liability and its go forward earnings should be higher too, at least in theory. How much of the reduced tax rate will be passed along to Berkshire's customers, through for instance, lower electricity rates or lower railroad shipping rates and how much will go to Berkshire's shareholders?

Warren: The question is, in the case of our utility businesses, all benefit of lower tax rates goes to customers and it should be, because we are allowed a return on equity, in general, I'm simplifying a little bit. We're allowed a return on equity that is computed on an after-tax basis and the utility commissions, would, if taxes were raised, would presumable give us higher rates to compensate for that. If taxes were lowered they would say, you're not entitled to make more money just because tax rates have been lowered. So, forget about the utility portion of the deferred taxes.

The deferred taxes that are applicable to our unrealized gains in securities, we would get all the benefit of, because I mentioned we had $90 billion plus of unrealized gains and if the rates were changed on those, in either direction, our owners, dollar for dollar will participate in that. Then you get into the other businesses, you mentioned the railroad particularly, but it could be all of our other businesses.

To some extent, if tax rates are lowered, to different degrees and different industries, depending on the number of players, the competitive conditions, some of it almost certainly gets competed away and some of it would likely not be competed away. Economist can argue about that a lot, but I've seen it in action, in a lot of cases. You got a big decline in rates, for example in the U.K., and we've had them over my lifetime. We had 52% corporate rates; we've had a lot of different numbers. So, I have seen how economic behavior works. I would say that it's certain that some of any lower rate would be competed away and it's virtually certain that some would go to the benefit of the shareholders. It is very industry and company specific in how that plays out. Charlie?

With dollar for dollar, I mean, there's 90 or 95 billion and if the rate were to drop 10%, by 10 percentage points, that 9 ½ billion is real. On the other hand, if it goes up, as it did, it went up 28 to 35%, they can take it away from us to.

Charlie: Well, I think it's true that we are peculiar in one way. If things go to hell in a handbasket and then get better later, we're likely to do better than most others. We don't wish for that and we don't want our country to have to suffer through it and we fear what might happen if the country went through the wringer like that. If that real adversity comes, we're likely to do better in the end. We're good at navigating through that kind of stuff. In fact, we're quite good at it.

Warren: There will be occasional hiccups in the American economy. It doesn't have much to do with who is President or anything like that. Those people might get blamed or given credit for different things. It's just the nature of market systems to occasionally go haywire, in one direction or another. It's not on a regular sine wave type picture or anything of the sort, but it's certain to happen from time to time and we will probably have a fair amount of money and credit at that time. We're certainly not affected. When the rest of world is fearful, we know America will come out fine. We will not have any trouble psychologically acting at all. The question is how much do we have in the way of resources? We'll also never put the company in any kind of risk just because we see a lot of opportunities. We'll grab all the ones we can handle and not lose a day of sleep.

[someone said something] I didn't quite get that. In any events, we will now go to Station 4.

BUFFETT SELLING DEPRECIATING ASSETS

Q12. Audience, Station 4: Dr. Bruce Hertz, from Glenview, Illinois. I wanted to thank you for allowing me to attend, I feel both honored and blessed. My question for Mr. Buffett is – you've always advised us to purchase equities that appreciate in value, yet a few years ago, you sold your used Cadillac at a tremendous profit. How can you justify selling a depreciating asset for a significant profit? Thank you.

Warren: Actually, I gave it to Girls Inc. and they sold it. It was kind of interesting [applause]. A very nice guy bought it for about $100,000 plus and Girls Inc. got the money. He came later actually with his family and he drove it away without any plates, he was driving back to New York and he got picked up by the police in Illinois. He started giving this explanation about how he'd given this money to Girls Inc. and was driving the car back and he had this nice looking family with him and the cops were quite skeptical. Fortunately, I had signed the dashboard for him as part of the deal. So, they looked at that and then they just said, did he give you any stocks tips and then they let him go. [laughter]. I can't recall ever selling a used car at a profit. I don't think I have sold any personal possessions. Well, I have a house for sale.

Charlie: You don't have any personal possessions. [laughter].

Warren: Anything you see with a figure attached like that.

Charlie: You are a fatter version of Mahatma Gandhi.

Warren: The guy was a very nice guy who bought it and his cheque cleared and so we were fine.

Becky?

INVESTING IN INDEX FUND

Q13. Journalist, Becly Quick: I like to ask a question that can serve as a follow up to the question that Carol had asked. Charlie in that response said that he thinks the Berkshire businesses on the whole would do better than the S&P 500. Clark Cameron, from Birmingham, Alabama, who owns 281 shares is Berkshire B, writes in and asks, why have you advised your wife to invest in index funds after your death rather than Berkshire Hathaway? I believe Munger has counselled his offspring to quote "not be so dumb as to sell".

Warren: She won't be selling any Berkshire to buy the index funds. All of my Berkshire, every single share will go to philanthropy. I don't even regard myself as owning Berkshire, basically. It's committed. [applause]. So far, about 40% of that has already been distributed.

So, the question is, somebody who is not an investment professional, will be, I hope, reasonably elderly by the time that the estate gets settled and what is the best investment – meaning one that there will be less worry of any kind connected with, and less people coming around and saying, why don't you sell this and do something else and all those things. She is going to have more money than she needs and the big thing you want then is for money not to be a problem. There will be no way, that if she holds the S&P, virtually no way, absent if something happens with weapons of mass destruction, but virtually no way, ... she will have all the money that she can possibly can use. She will have a little liquid money so that if stocks are down tremendously at some point, or if they close the stock exchange for a while, or anything like that, she will still feel that she has plenty of money. The object is not to maximize. It doesn't make any difference whether the amount she gets doubles or triples or anything of the sort. The important thing is that she never worries about money the rest of her life.

I had an aunt Katy here in Omaha, Charlie knew well, who worked for her husband, as did I and she worked hard all her life and had lived in a house she paid $8,000 for, 45th and Hickory all her life. Because she was in Berkshire (she lived until she was 97), she ended up with a few hundred million and she would write me a letter every four or five months and she said, "Dear Warren, I hate to bother you, but am I going to run out of money?" I would write her back and say, "Dear Katy, it's a good question because if you lived 986 years, you're going to run out of money." Then about four or five months later, she would write me the same letter again. There is no way in the world that if you have plenty of money, that it should become a minus in your life. There will be people, if you got a lot of money, that would come around with various suggestions for you, sometimes well meaning, sometimes not so well meaning. So, if you have something that is certain to deliver, if it was all in Berkshire, they would say "well if Warren was alive today, he would be telling you to do this..." and I just don't want anyone to go through that. So, I think actually what I am suggesting is what a very high percentage of people should do, or something like that. I don't think there is a chance they would have as much peace of mind, if they own one stock and they got neighbors and friends and relatives that are trying to induce him, like I said, sometimes with well intentions and sometimes otherwise to do something else. So, I think it's a policy that will get a good result and is likely to stick.

Charlie?

Charlie: Well as Becky said, "the Mungers are different." I want them to hold the Berkshire.

Warren: Well, I want to hold Berkshire too.

Charlie: I recognize the logic that S&P algorithm is very hard to beat. You know the diversified portfolio of big companies is all but impossible for most people. I'm just more comfortable with the Berkshire.

Warren: It's the family business. I've seen too many people as they get older particularly, just having to listen to the arguments of people.

Charlie: Well if you're going to protect your heirs from the stupidity of others, you may have some good system, but I'm not much interested in that subject. [laughter].

Warren: OK, Jay.

KRAFT-HEINZ AND UNILEVER DEAL

Q14. Analyst, Jay Gelb: Berkshire reportedly partnered with 3G in Kraft-Heinz's attempt to acquire Unilever for $143 billion. How much was Berkshire willing to invest in this deal and does this mean Berkshire's next large acquisition is likely to be in partnership with 3G?

Warren: You have to distinguish between two situations. Kraft-Heinz was a widely-owned company in which we and 3G act as a control group and have a little over 50% of the stock. But, as originally contemplated, most certainly, this is exactly what would have happened, we would've invested an additional $15 billion and 3G would've invested an additional $15 billion, if a friendly agreement could have been reached. So, if the deal had been made, if the independent directors of Kraft-Heinz had approved the transaction, then the likelihood is we would have invested $15 billion, but it would have required the approval of the independent directors as well. Now, Kraft-Heinz in going forward with making that offer, wanted to be sure there would be enough equity capital in addition to the debt that would be incurred to make the deal. So, informally, we basically committed the $15 billion. It only was approved on the basis that it would be a friendly deal with Unilever. Initially we thought they would be, at least possibly interested in such a deal and when we found out otherwise, we withdrew the offer. So, it would have been $15 billion of additional money, in all probability.

OK, Station 5.

TEACHING VALUE INVESTING

Q15. Audience, Station 5: Dear honorable Mr. Buffett and Mr. Munger, I'm Kenda Hua from China. My company Kyat Holdings is spreading value investing philosophy in Asia. My business partners Ken Chi, Joe Cui and I are committed to awake 100 million Chinese people to return to rational way of investing. The hardest thing in this world is to change people's values or belief system, and we should like to awake investors to change from speculating in the market to investing in the market. It's not changing the speculators' values or their belief systems. May I ask you, Mr. Buffett, can you kindly advise us what we should do, to spread your value investing philosophy, or is there any word of encouragement? Thank You.

Warren: In any system, Keynes wrote about this in 1936 I think it was, in The General Theory 30 or 35, chapter 12, great chapter on investing. He talked about investment and speculation and the propensity of people to speculate and the dangers of it and worded eloquently. There is always the possibility, I mean there is always some speculation obviously and there is always some value investors and that sort of thing in the market. When speculation gets rampant and when you're getting, I guess Charlie would call it "social proof", that has worked recently, people can get very excited about speculating in markets and we will have it from time to time in this market. There's nothing more agonizing than to see your neighbor, who you think has an IQ of about 30 points below you, getting richer than you are, by buying stocks, whether it's Internet stocks or whatever. People succumb to that and they will succumb in this economy just as elsewhere. There is also a point which gets to your question - I would say that early on in the development of markets, there is probably some tendency for them, I think, to be more speculative than markets that have been around for a couple of hundred years. Markets have a casino characteristic that has a lot of appeal to people particularly when they see, like when people are getting rich around them. And those who haven't been through cycles before are probably a little more prone to speculate than people who have experienced the outcome of wild speculations.

Basically, in this country, Ben Graham was, in the book I read in 1949, preaching investment and that book continues to sell very well. But if the markets get hot and new issues are doing well, and people on leverage are doing well, a lot of people will be attracted to, not only speculation, but what I would call gambling and I'm afraid that will be true in the United States. But I think that China, being a newer market, essentially in which there is widespread participation, is likely to have some pretty extreme experiences in that respect. We will have some in this country too. Charlie?

Charlie: Well I certainly agree with that. The Chinese will have more trouble. They are very bright people and have a lot of action and sure they are going to be more speculative. And it's a dumb idea. To the extent you're working on it, you're on the side of the angels, but lots of luck. [laughter].

Warren: It will offer the investor more opportunities actually, if they can keep their wits about them. If you have wild speculation, Charlie just mentioned earlier, if we get into periods that are very tough, Berkshire certainly will do reasonably well because we won't get fearful. Fear spreads like you cannot believe until you've seen a few examples of it. At the start of September 2008, you had 35 million people with their money in money market funds, with 3 ½ trillion dollars in them and none of them were afraid that that dollar wasn't going to be a dollar when they went to cash in their money market funds and three weeks later they were all terrified and the $175 billion flowed out in three days. So, the way the public can react is really extreme in markets, and that actually offers opportunities for investors. People like action and they like to gamble and if they think there's easy money to be made, a lot of them, you'll get a rush to it and for a while it will be self-fulfilling and create new converts until the day of reckoning comes.

Just keep preaching, investing, and if the market swings around a lot, you'll keep adding a few people here and there to a group that recognizes that markets are there to be taken advantage of rather than to instruct you as to what is going on.

OK, Andrew. You want to add anything, Charlie?

Charlie: We have done a lot of preaching Warren without much effect.

Warren: Right and that's probably good, from my standpoint. Ok, Andrew.

INVESTMENT TAX CREDIT AND ITS IMPACT ON BNSF

Q16. Journalist, Andrew Ross Sorkin: Thank you Warren. This question comes from Ryan Prince. President Donald Trump and his advisors have talked about proposing a substantial investment tax credit, to provide incentives for long term corporate fixed capital investment. In BNSF, Berkshire owns a sprawling infrastructure portfolio requiring regular routine maintenance investment of substantial scale. What impact would an investment tax credit have on BNSF's capital investment decision making, from a return on investment capital perspective, as well as in terms of timing and, just as importantly, given the current economy and employment picture, would such a tax credit amount to a subsidization of otherwise mandatory maintenance capital investment, or a proper incentive to stimulate investment?

Warren: Well it would all depend on how it was worded, because we've had investment tax credits in this country and we had bonus depreciations, another form of it and we do get extra first year depreciation. That does not enter into our calculation very much. In fact, certainly at the Berkshire level, I've never instructed anybody to do anything different because of investment tax credit or accelerated depreciation. There may be some calculations done down at the operating company level.

It's certainly true in something like the wind projects and solar projects – they are dependent on the tax law currently. There may come a time when they aren't, but they wouldn't have been done without some subsidization through the tax law. I would say if you changed the depreciation schedules and double depreciation, triple depreciation, that we are going to do what we need to do at the railroad to make it safer and more efficient if we just had ordinary depreciation. I doubt there would be any dramatic differences. Obviously, if you were going to, say, buy a bunch of planes and the law was going to change on December 31st and the math made it better to wait until January 1st, or do it this December 31st, you would make this type of calculation.

I can't recall in all the years that I have ever sent out anything to our managers, saying let's do this because the tax law is being changed, or might be changed or something of the sort. As I mentioned earlier, it changes just a little bit if you think there is going to be a change in capital gains rates, at a given time. Obviously, if the rate is going to be lowered you would take losses ahead of time and defer gains may be a little, and that is why it is useful. Actually, if the tax committees in the Senate and the House are working on something, it might be useful if the Chairman would say that "if we do make any changes we're likely to use this effective date" or something of the sort and I think they have done that a few times in the past.

The big tax driven item is in wind and solar and that is a specific policy, because the government has decided they want to move people - or society has decided they want to move people towards those forms of electric generation and the market system wouldn't do it. There may come a time when the market system will do it all by itself. We won't make big changes and it's so speculative anyway in terms of even what the law would be. Beyond that, if it becomes less speculative as the law may really look like something is going to be different, it doesn't change this big time at all.

Charlie?

Charlie: Nothing to add. We're not going to change anything at Berkshire, at the railroad, for some little tax jiggle.

Warren: If we need a bridge repaired, we're going to repair the bridge. We need a lot of track maintenance all the time and that sort of thing. I don't think Matt and I have ever had a talk about it since we've owned the railroad.

Gregg.

COAL AND GROWTH IN BNSF

Q17. Analyst, Gregg Warren: Warren, my question also relates to Burlington Northern. Despite the current administration's belief that they can bring the coal industry back, market forces continue to lead to the industry's demise. While 90 percent of U.S. coal consumption is driven by electricity generation, natural gas has been both cheaper and cleaner burning and renewable electricity generation has remade parts of the market, as wind and solar have gained scale and become cheaper alternatives. This has created problems for Burlington Northern, with coal shipments accounting for just 18 percent of volume and revenue last year, down from an average of 24 percent for both measures the previous ten years. While some of this was due to a large buildup of coal supplies the past couple of winters, which finally seem to be working their way out, what are your expectations for the contribution coal can make to BNSF longer term? I know the rail will currently handle some export shipments going through Canada's Pacific coast ports, but will there be enough growth there to offset domestic demand, or will BNSF need to rely more heavily on segments like intermodal to offset lost coal volumes?

Warren: The answer is coal is going to go down over time and I don't think there is much question about that. The specifics of any given year relate, very importantly, to the price of natural gas. Right now, the demand is somewhat up, fair amount up from last year because natural gas is at \$3.15 or

$3.20 and the utilities can produce electricity, in many cases, quite a bit cheaper with coal than with natural gas; whereas if it were $2, it would be natural gas. But over time coal, in my mind, is essentially certain to decline as a percentage of the revenue of the railroad. The speed at which it does – you don't build great generation plants overnight. So, you can't predict the rate and if natural gas is cheap enough, you'll see a big conversion back to natural gas. Coal is going to go down as a percentage of revenues significantly. Certainly over 10 years it will be quite significant and who knows exactly year by year. We are looking for other sources of growth than coal. If you're tied to coal, you've got problems.

Charlie?

Charlie: Well, if you go out for the extremely long term, I think that all hydrocarbons will be used, including all the coal. So, I think that in the end, these hydrocarbons are a huge resource for humanity and I don't think we've got any good substitutes. I never minded saving them for the next generation. I don't like using them up very fast. I am often on the road on my own on this one. People think that all these hydrocarbons are going to be stranded and the whole world is going to change, but I think we are going to use every drop of the hydrocarbons sooner or later. We'll use them as chemical feedstocks. I regard all these things as very hard to predict and I'm not at all sure of it. I would eventually expect natural gas to be pretty short in supply.

Warren: A change in storage would make a big difference. We will produce, within a few years, as much electricity in Iowa, or virtually as much electricity in Iowa from wind as our customers use, but the wind only blows about 35% of the time, or something like that and sometimes it blows too hard. But the storage, having it 24 hours a day, seven days a week is a real problem even if we've got the capability of producing, like I say, a self-sufficient amount essentially in Iowa before very long.

Our shipments of coal are fairly substantial this year on the BNSF, but they were very low last year and, as you said, stockpiles grew and have come down somewhat. They are still on the high side. But, in my mind, ... Charlie has got a longer-term outlook on this. In my mind, we're going to be shipping a whole lot less coal 10 or 20 years from now than we are now. On the other hand, I think there are some decent prospects in other long hauls. I mean it's a pretty cheap way to move bulk commodities long distance - rail is. And I think it's a good business but the coal aspect of it is going to diminish.

OK, Station 6.

INVESTMENT IN CAPITAL-LIGHT COMPANIES

Q18. Audience, Station 6: Good morning. It's Marcus Burns from Sydney, Australia. My question to Mr. Buffett is, you used to buy capital-light, cash generative businesses, but now buy lower growth capital consumptive businesses. I realize Berkshire generates a little cash flow, but would shareholders have been better off if you had continued to invest in capital-light companies?

Warren: Well, we'd love to find them. There's no question that buying a high return on assets, very light capital intensive business is going to grow and beats the hell out of buying something that requires a lot of capital to grow. And this varies from day to day and I don't think it's sufficiently appreciated.

I believe that probably the five largest American companies by market cap — and some days we're in that group and some days we aren't (let's assume we're not in that group) – on a given day, they have a market value of over $2.5 trillion, and that $2.5 trillion is a big number. I don't know what the aggregate market cap of the U.S. market is, but that's probably getting up close to 10% of the whole market cap of the United States. If you take those five companies, essentially you could run them with no equity capital at all, none. That is a very different world than when Andrew Carnegie was building a steel mill and then using the earnings to build another steel mill and getting very rich in the process. Or, Rockefeller was building refineries and buying tank cars.

Generally speaking, for a very long time in our capitalism, growing and earning large amounts of money required considerable reinvestment of capital and large amounts of equity capital, the railroads being a good example. That world has really changed and I don't think people quite appreciate the difference. You literally don't need any money to run the five companies that are worth collectively more than $2.5 trillion and who have outpaced any number of those names that were familiar if you looked at the Fortune 500 list, 30 or 40 years ago, whether it was Exxon or General Motors, you name it. So, we would love, I mean there is no question that a business that doesn't take any capital and grows and has almost infinite returns on required equity capital is the ideal business. And we own a couple of businesses, a few businesses that earn extraordinary returns on capital but they don't grow. We still love them, but if were in fields that would grow, believe me, they would be number one on our list. We aren't seeing those that we can buy and we understand well. You are absolutely right, that's a far far far better way of laying out money than what we are able to do when buying capital-intensive businesses.

Charlie?

Charlie: The chemical companies of America at one time

were wonderful investments. Dow and DuPont sold at 20 something earnings and they kept building more and more complicated plants and hiring more PhD chemists and it looked like they owned the world. Now most chemical products are sort of commoditized and it's a tough business being a big chemical producer. In comes other people like Apple and Google and they're just on top of the world. I think the questioner is basically right, that the world has changed a lot and that the people who have made the right decisions in getting into these new businesses that are so different from the old ones have done very well.

Warren: Andrew Mellon would be, actually, baffled by looking at the high-cap companies now. I mean the idea that you could create hundreds of billions of value, essentially without assets, without tangible assets.

Charlie: Fast

Warren: Fast, yeah, but that is the world. I mean when Google can sell you something, where GEICO was paying $11 or something every time someone clicked something, that is a lot different than spending years finding the right site and developing iron mines to supply the steel plants and railroads to haul the iron to where the steel is produced and distribution points and all that sort of thing. Our world was built, when we first looked at it, our U.S. capitalist system, basically was built on tangible assets and reinvestments and that sort of thing and a lot of innovation and invention to go with it. But this is so much better if you happen to be good at it: to essentially be able to build hundreds of billions of market value without really needing any capital. That is a different world than existed in the past and I think it's a world that's likely to continue. I don't think the trend in that direction is over by a long shot.

Charlie: A lot of the people who are chasing that thing very hard now, in the venture capital field are losing a lot of money. It's a wonderful field, but not everybody is going to win big in it; a few are going to win big in it.

Warren: Ok, Carol?

VALUE OF BERKSHIRE TO THE WORLD

Q19. Journalist, Carol Loomis: This question is from a shareholder in California in the Silicon Valley area, who didn't want his name mentioned because he said he wasn't looking for publicity, but whose picture makes him appear to be a millennial. Every Berkshire shareholder knows about the stock market value of Berkshire, but my question is about the value of Berkshire to the world. For instance, the value of Apple to the world has been iPhones. The value of GEICO is cost effective auto insurance. The value of 3G (and I will tell you that there are some shareholders who would be arguing about here) but the value of 3G is improved operations. But about Berkshire, I just don't know, in managing Berkshire subsidiaries, as Mr. Munger once famously said, you practice delegation just short of abdication, so hands on management can't be the answer. That means the majority of Berkshire's subsidiaries would do just as well if they were to stay independent companies. So that's my question, what is the value of Berkshire to the world?

Warren: Well, I would say the question about, … I'm with him to the point which he accurately describes as delegation to the point of abdication. But I would argue that, that abdication actually in many cases, will enable those businesses to be run better than they would if they were part of the S&P 500 and the target perhaps of activists, or somebody who wants to get some kind of a jiggle in the short term. So, I think that our abdication actually has some very positive value on the companies. You would have to look at it company by company.

We've got probably 50 managers in attendance here. Naturally, they are not going to say anything publicly or on television or anything where they knock us or anything, but get them off in a private corner somewhere and ask them whether they think their business can be run better with a management by abdication from Berkshire, but with also all the capital strengths of Berkshire, that with any project that makes sense can be funded in a moment without worrying whether the banks are still lending like in 2008, or whether Wall Street will applaud it or something of that sort. So, I think our hands-off style, actually I think, can add significant value in many companies. We do have managers here you could ask about that. We certainly don't add to value by calling them up and saying that we've developed a better system, for turning up additives at Lubrizol or running GEICO better than Tony Nicely can run it or anything of the sort.

We have a very objective view about capital allocation. We can free managers up... I would say that we might very well free up, at least 20% of the time of a CEO in the normal public company - who otherwise would have a public company, just in terms of meeting with analysts and the calls, dealing with banks and all kinds of things that essentially we relieve them of so that they can spend all of their time figuring out the best way to run their business. So, I think that we bring something to the party - even if we are just sitting there with our feet up on the desk.

Charlie?

Charlie: We're trying to be a good example for the world. I don't think we'd be having these big shareholder meetings if there weren't a little bit of teaching ethos in Berkshire and I have watched it closely for a long time. I'd argue that, that's what we are trying to do: to set a proper example, stay sane, and be honest. [applause]. So, I'm proud of Berkshire and I don't worry too much if we sell Coca-Cola.

Warren: I would say GEICO is an extraordinarily well-run company and it would be extraordinarily well run if it were public. But it has gone from 2 and a fraction percent of the auto insurance market to 12% and part of the reason, a small part (the real key is GEICO and Tony Nicely) but part of the reason is that when other − at least two of our competitors − big competitors said that they would not meet their profit objectives, if they didn't lighten up their interest in new business eight or ten months ago. I think our business decision to step on the gas is a better business decision. But I think that GEICO as a public company would have more trouble making that decision than they do when their part of GEICO, because we are thinking about nothing but where GEICO is going to be in about 5 or 10 years. We want new business cost to capitalize our earnings in the short term, and other people have different pressures. I'm not arguing about how they behave, because they have a different constituency than GEICO has with Berkshire and what Berkshire has with its shareholders in turn. I think that our system is superior, but it's not because we work harder; Charlie and I hardly do anything.

Jonathan?

PERIODIC PAYMENT ANNUITY BUSINESS

Q20. Analyst, Jonathan Brandt: Could you please talk about your periodic payment annuity business? The weighted average interest rate on these contracts is 4.1 percent, which doesn't sound particularly attractive given the current interest rate environment. Is the duration of these liabilities long enough to make that an attractive

cost of funds, or were these contracts executed primarily when rates were higher?

Warren: Well, these contracts – those are what you would call structured settlements primarily. When somebody young has a terrible auto accident or whatever it may be, perhaps urged by the court, or urged by family members who really do have the interest of the injured party at heart, they may convert what could be a large sum settlement, probably against the insurance company, you know may be a million dollars or maybe two million dollars, into periodic payments for the rest of the life of the injured party and we issue those for other insurance companies. In fact, sometimes the court directs that Berkshire, or hints strongly that Berkshire should be the one to issue those, because you're talking about somebody's life 30 or 40 or 50 years from now and the court, or the lawyer or the family, they want to be very very sure that whoever makes that promise is going to be around to keep it and Berkshire has a preferred position in that. To get to your question, Jonny, we look to taking the longer maturity situations, we always have, and we have to make assumptions about mortality and then we have to decide what interest rate will do it. The 4.1 is a mix of a lot of contracts over a lot of years, obviously. We write maybe 30 million of these, about 20 to 30 million a week, looking for the long maturities. So, if you take an average of 15 years or something of the sort, that's how we come up with that sort of a figure. We adjust to interest rates at all times and when doing that we're making an assumption that we're going to earn more money than is inherent in the cost of these structured settlements. It's a business we've, I think we've got 6 or 7 billion of now and we'll keep doing them. Incidentally, probably a significant percentage of the 6 or 7 billion we're not yet paying anything on, somebody else may have the earlier payments, they're certainly weighted far out. So, it's a business that we'll be in 10 or 20 years from now.

We've got some natural advantage because people trust us more than any other company to make those payments and the test is whether we earn, overtime, a return above that, which we're paying to the injured party and that's a bet we're willing to make. But if interest rates continued at the present levels for a long time, we would, assuming we kept the money in fixed income instruments, we'd have some loss in it. We've got an allowance in there for the expenses incidentally because we do make monthly payments to these people eventually and we have to keep track of whether they are still alive or not, because you cannot count on some of the relatives of somebody that is deceased, when a cheque is coming in every month to notify you promptly that the person has become deceased. That number will go up over time. If interest rates stay where they are, that 4.1 will come down a little bit as we add new business.

OK, Station 7.

"I've avoided all my life compensation consultants. To me, I hardly can find the words to express my contempt… I think there's a lot of mumbo jumbo in this field, and I don't see it going away."
Charlie Munger

"People are going to have 120 IQ or 140 IQ or whatever it may be, very similar scoring abilities in terms of intelligence tests and some of them have minds that are good at one kind of thing and some of another. And I've known very bright people that do not have money minds and they can make very unintelligent decisions they can do all kinds of other things that most mortals can't do… It isn't the way their wiring works."
Warren Buffett

"Capitalism is the golden goose that we all live on. And if people generally get so they have contempt for it because they don't like the pay arrangements in the system, your capitalism may not last as well. And that's like killing the golden goose."
Charlie Munger

INVESTMENT IN USG CORP.

Q21. Audience, Station 7: Thank you, Mr. Buffett and Mr. Munger for all you have done and the opportunity to learn even more from your approach to investing in life. My name is Harry Hong and I'm a respirologist from Vancouver, British Columbia. The question involves back in 2001, you made an initial investment in USG shortly before the company declared bankruptcy, due to the mounting asbestos liability. You held those shares through the bankruptcy process even though standard wisdom says that the equity in Chapter 11 is usually worthless. Can you explain why USG's equity was a safe investment?

Warren: Well I don't really remember all the details then.

Charlie: It was very cheap, very cheap.

Warren: I would say this, USG, we owned I'm not sure what percentage, but it's a very significant percentage...

Charlie: 20% or something.

Warren: Probably 30% or something like that. USG, overall, has been disappointing because the gypsum business has been disappointing. I may be wrong, but I think they went bankrupt twice. First, from asbestos going back and then subsequently because they had too much debt. So, it has not been a brilliant investment. Now if gypsum prices were at levels that they were in some years in the past, it would have worked out a lot better.

Charlie: It hasn't been terrible.

Warren: No, it hasn't been terrible. But gypsum took a real dive several times and there has been too much gypsum capacity and then when it comes back, managements have been, not as early at USG, but including USG perhaps, they got more optimistic about future demands than they should have. They like, going back the historically, they like to build new plants and it's a business where the supply – the potential supply has been significantly greater than demand in a lot of years. I mean, you've seen housing starts since 2008 and 2009 not come back anywhere near as much as people anticipated. So, gypsum prices have moved up but not dramatically, so just put that one down as not one of our great ideas, not one of my great ideas, Charlie wasn't involved in that. It's no disaster though.

Charlie: No, it isn't.

Warren: Becky?

AJIT JAIN AND INSURANCE BUSINESS

Q22. Journalist, Becky Quick: This question comes from Axel Myerseek in Germany, who writes, if Ajit Jain were to retire, God forbid be promoted, what would be the impact on the insurance operations, both with regards to underwriting profit as well as the development of float?

Warren: Well, nobody will or could possibly replace Ajit. I mean you just can't come close. But we have a terrific operation in insurance, we really do, outside of Ajit. And it's terrific, squared with Ajit. There are things only he can do, but there are a lot of things that are institutionalized, a lot of things in our insurance business, where we got extraordinarily able management too. So, Ajit for example, bought a company that nobody here has heard of probably called Guard Insurance a few years ago. Based, (workers comp primarily), it's based in - probably in - Wilkes-Barre, Pennsylvania and it's expanding like crazy in Wilkes-Barre. It's been a gem and Ajit oversees it. But we've got a terrific person running it. We bought Medical Protective some years ago, Tim Kenesey runs that, Ajit oversees it. But Tim Kenesey can run a terrific insurance company with or without Ajit. But he's smart enough to realize that if he's got somebody like Ajit willing to oversee it to a degree, that's great. But Tim is a great insurance manager all by himself and Medical Protective has been a wonderful business for us and most people don't know we own it. The company goes back to the 19th century, actually.

We've got a lot of good operations. If you look at that section in the Annual Report called "other insurance company," I mean that is, in aggregate, that is a wonderful insurance company and there is very few like it. GEICO is a terrific company. So, Ajit has made more money for Berkshire than I have probably but we've still got what I would consider the world's best property casualty insurance operation even without him and with him I don't think anybody comes close.

Charlie?

Charlie: A few years ago, California made a little change in its workers' compensation law and Ajit saw instantly that it would cause the underwriting results to change drastically, and he went from a tiny percent of the market, bought 10% of the market which is big and he just grasped a couple of billion dollars, at least, out of the air, like it was like snapping his fingers and when it got tough he pulled back. We don't have a lot of people like Ajit. It's hard to just snap your fingers and grab a couple of billion dollars out of the air. [laughter as Warren Buffett snaps his fingers in the air].

Warren: Actually, the California workers' comp though, Guard has moved into that. We have got a lot of terrific insurance managers. I mean, I don't know of a better collection any place and Ajit has found some of those. I've gotten lucky a few times. I mean Tom Nerney at U.S. Liability, that goes back about 15 or 16 years. He has a terrific operation, not huge, but is so well managed and people don't even know we own these things. You look at that last line and now we've added Peter Eastwood with Berkshire Hathaway Specialty and these are really good businesses, I got to tell you.

When you can produce underwriting profits and on top of that just hand more float, we don't have any businesses like that. Those are great businesses. We've got 100 or whatever it is, $100 billion plus of money that we get to earn on, while at the same time, overall, on balance we're likely to make some additional money for holding them. If you can get someone to hand you $104 billion and pay you to hold it, while you get to invest and get the proceeds it's a good business. Now most people don't do well at it. The problem is what I just described tempts lots of people to get into it and recently people have got into it really just for the investment management as a way to earn money offshore. We don't do that but it can be done for small companies with investment management. So, there's a lot of competition there. But, we have some fundamental advantages, plus we have, short in areas, plus we have absolutely terrific managers to maximize those advantages and we're going to make the most of it.

(I've just been handed something Kraft-Heinz came out with. They just came out with it commercially a couple of days ago, maybe a few weeks ago. At the directors meeting they had this, I had three of these. I'm sure that there's a member or two of the audience that may not approve of it. [laughter]. But I got to tell you, folks, it's good. It's a cheesecake arrangement with topping and Philadelphia cream cheese, so you can create your own cheesecake and I thought that I could eat it while Charlie is talking and you'll be able to get it at the half time. It's selling very well and I think, just so you don't feel too guilty - it's 170 calories for this cherry one and like I said I've had three of these and I don't mind having 5 or 600 calories for dessert. I'll let somebody else eat the broccoli and I'll have the dessert. So, we will be eating this, and you too at half time. I think they brought 8 or 9000 of these. I will be disappointed if we don't run out. Actually, I will be disappointed at you, not them.

Ok, Jay.

SUCCESSION PLANNING

Q23. Analyst, Jay Gelb: This question is on the topic of succession planning. Warren, there seems to be fewer mentions by name of top performing Berkshire managers in this year's annual letter. Does this mean you are changing your message regarding the succession plan for Berkshire's next CEO?

Warren: Well the answer to that is no and I didn't realize that there were fewer mentions by name. I write that thing out and send it to Carol and she tells me to go back to work. I don't actually think that much about how many personnel get named. I would say this, and this is absolutely true, we have never had more good managers, that's because we have more good companies, but we have never had more good managers than what we have now. But it has nothing to do with succession.

Charlie?

Charlie: Well, I certainly agree with that. We don't seem to have a whole lot of 20 year olds.

Warren: Certainly, not at the front table. We've got an extraordinary group of good managers, which is why we can manage by abdication. It wouldn't work if we had a whole bunch of people who had come with the idea of getting my job. If we had 50 people out there, all who wanted to be running Berkshire Hathaway, it would not work very well. They have the jobs they want in life.

Tony Nicely loves running GEICO. You could have a line, they have jobs they love and that's a lot better in my view than having a whole bunch of them out there that are kind of doing their job and they are kind of hoping that the guy they are competing with fails, so that when I'm not around they'll get the nod. It's a much different system than exists in most large American corporations.

Charlie, you got anything?

OK, we will go to Station 8.

BULLISH/BEARISH SECTORS

Q24. Audience, Station 8: Hi Warren and Charlie, my name is Vicky Wei. I'm a MBA student from the Wharton School of Business. This is my first time to be in the meeting. I'm really excited about it. Thanks for having us here.

Warren: Thanks for coming.

Audience: My question is where do you want to go fishing for the next 3 to 5 years? Which sectors are you most bullish on and which sectors are you most bearish on? Thank you.

Warren: Charlie and I do not really discuss sectors much, nor do we let the macro environment, or thoughts about it enter into our decisions. We are really opportunistic and we obviously are indulging in all kinds of businesses all the time. It's a hobby with us almost, probably more with me than Charlie. But we are hoping that we'll get a call, we've got a bunch of filters, and I would say to the both of us, we probably know in the first 5 minutes or less, whether something is likely to ... or has a reasonable chance of happening. It's just going to go through there and the first question is, can we really ever know enough about this to come to a decision? That knocks out a whole bunch of things, and there's a few, and then if it makes it through there. There's a pretty good reasonable chance that we're going to do something, but it's not sector specific.

We do love the companies obviously, with the moats around the product, where consumer behavior can be perhaps predicted further out. But I would say it's getting harder, for us anyway, to anticipate consumer behavior than what we might have thought 20 or 30 years ago. I think it's just a tougher game now. But, we'll measure it and we'll look at it in terms of returns on present capital and returns on prospective capital. A lot of people give you some signals as to what kind of people they are, even in talking for the first 5 minutes and whether you're likely to actually have a satisfactory arrangement with them over time. So, a lot of things go on fast. But we know the kind of sectors we kind of like or the type of business we kind of like to end up in, but we don't really say we're going to go after companies in this field or that field or another field.

Charlie, you want to ... ?

Charlie: Yeah, some of our subsidiaries do little bolt-on acquisitions that make sense, and that goes on all the time and, of course, we like it. But I would say the general field of buying whole companies, it's gotten very competitive. There's a huge industry of doing these leveraged buyouts, that's what I still call them. The people who do them think that's kind of a bad marker. So, they say they do private equity; you know, it's like may be a janitor calling himself chief of engineering or something. But anyway, the people who do the leveraged buyouts, they can finance practically anything in about a week or so through shadow banking and they can pay very high prices and get very good terms. So, it's very very hard to buy businesses. We've done well because there's a certain small group of people that don't want to sell to private equity, and they love the business so much they don't want to just dress it up for resale.

Warren: We had a guy some years ago came to see me and he was 61 at the time and he said look, I've got a fine business. I got all the money I could possibly need, but he said there's only one thing that worries me when I drive to work. Actually, there's more than one guy who's told me that, that has used the same term. There's only one thing that bothers me when I drive to work, something happens to me today, my wife is left, you know I've seen these cases where executives in the company try to buy them out cheap or they sell to a competitor, ... all the people .... He said, "I don't want to leave her with the business. I want to decide where it goes, but I want to keep running it and I love it. And he said, I thought about selling it to a competitor. But if I sell it to a competitor, their CFO is going to become the CFO of the new company and on down the line, all those people who helped me build the business, a lot of them are going to get dumped and I will walk away with a ton of money and some of them will lose their jobs. He said I don't want to do that. He said I can sell it to a leveraged buyout firm, who prefer to call themselves private equity, but they're going to leverage it to the hilt and then they're going to resell it and dress it up some. But in the end it's not going to be in the same place. I don't know where it's going to go, so I don't want to do that."

He said, it isn't because you're so special, he said there just isn't anyone else. If you're ever proposing to a potential spouse, don't use that line. But that's what he told me and I took it well and we made a deal. So logically, unless somebody has that attitude, we should lose in this market. I mean you can borrow so much money so cheap, and we're looking at the money as pretty much all equity capital and we're not competitive with somebody that's going to have a very significant portion of the purchased price carried in debt, maybe averaging 4% or something like that.

Charlie: And he won't take the losses if it goes down and he gets part of the profits if it goes up.

Warren: Its calculus is just so different than ours and he's got the money to make the deal. So, if all you care about is getting the highest price for your business, you know, we're not a good call and we will get some calls in any event and we can't offer something that, I wouldn't call it unique but it's unusual. The person who sold us that business and a couple of others, actually it's almost word for word the same thing they say, they are all happy with the sale they made, very happy and they have lots and lots and lots of money and are doing what they love doing, which is still running the business. They know that they made a decision that will leave their family and the people who worked for them all their lives, in the best possible position and that's in their equation. In their equation, they have done what's best. But that is not the equation of many people and it certainly isn't the equation of somebody who buys and borrows every dime they can, with the idea of re-selling it after they dress up the account and do some other things. But when the disparity gets so wide between what a heavily debt-financed purchase will bring as against what an equity type purchase will bring, it gets to be tougher, there's no question about it and it will stay that way.

Charlie: But it's been tough for a long time and we've bought some good businesses.

Warren: Ok, Andrew?

SUCCESSOR(S) COMPENSATION

Q25. Journalist, Andrew Ross Sorkin: Warren, this comes from a shareholder who, I think, is here but asked to remain anonymous, writes: "Three years ago, you were asked at the meeting about how you thought we should compensate your successor. You said it was a good question and you would address it in the next annual letter. We've been patiently waiting." [laughter]. "Can you tell us now, at least philosophically, how you've been thinking about the way the company should compensate your successor, so we don't have to worry when the pay consultants arrive on the scene?"

Warren: Well, unfortunately at my age I don't have to worry about things I said three years ago, but this guy, obviously much younger, remembers. I'll accept his word that I said that. There's a couple of possibilities, actually, but I don't want to get into details on them, but I actually would hope that we would have somebody: (a) he is already very rich, – which they should be. They've been working a long time and got that kind of ability and are very rich, and really is not motivated by whether they have 10 times as much money they and the families can need or a 100 times as much, and they might even wish to perhaps set an example by engaging for something far lower than, actually what you can say, their true market value is and that could or could not happen, but, I think it would be terrific if it did, but I can't blame anybody for wanting their market value. And if they didn't elect to go in that direction, I would say that you would probably pay them a very modest amount and then have an option which increased in striking price annually; nobody does this – hardly – Graham Holdings has done it. The Washington Post Company did a little bit, but would increase assuming that there was substantial retained earnings ever year, because, why should somebody retain a bunch of earnings and then claim they actually improved the value simply because they withheld the money from shareholders.

So, it's very easy to design that and in private companies, people do design it that way. They just don't want to do it in public companies because they get more money the other way. But they might have a very substantial one that could be exercised, but where the shares had to be held a couple of years after retirement, so that they really got the results, over time, that the majority of the stockholders would be able to get and not be able to pick their spots as to when they exercised and sold a lot of stock. It's not hard to design and it really depends who you're dealing with in terms of, actually, how much they care about money and having money beyond what they can possibly use. Most people do have an interest in that and I don't blame them. I don't know, what do you think Charlie?

Charlie: One thing I think is, I've avoided all my life compensation consultants. To me, I hardly can find the words to express my contempt. [laughter].

Warren: I would say this: if the board hires a compensation consultant after I go, I will come back. [laughter].

Charlie: Mad, mad. So, I think there's a lot of mumbo jumbo in this field, and I don't see it going away.

Warren: Oh, it isn't going to go away. No it's going to get worse. I mean if you look at the way compensation gets handled, you know, everybody looks at everybody else's proxy statement and says we can't possibly hire a guy that ... and so on.

Charlie: Its ridiculous.

Warren: The Human Relations department, you know, who work for the CEO come in and suggest a consultant. What consultant is ever going to get another assignment, that says you should pay your CEO below down the fourth quartile, because you're going to get a fourth quartile result. I mean it isn't that the people are evil or anything, it's just the nature of the situation. It produces a result that is not consistent with how representatives of the owners should behave.

Charlie: It's even worse than that. Capitalism is the golden goose that we all live on. And if people generally get so they have contempt for it because they don't like the pay arrangements in the system, your capitalism may not last as well. And that's like killing the golden goose. So, I think the existing system has a lot wrong with it.

Warren: I think there is something coming in pretty soon. I may be wrong about this where companies are going to have to put in their proxy statement what the CEO is paid relative to the average pay or something like that. That isn't going to change anything.

Charlie: It won't change a thing.

Warren: It won't change a thing.

Charlie: By the way, it will not get any headline either. It will tucked away.

Warren: And it will cost us a lot of money. With 367,000 people employed around world, I mean, we'll hope to get something that makes us somewhat similar so we can use estimates or something of the sort. But to get the median income or mean income or whatever or however the rules may read ...

Charlie: That's what consultants are for, Warren.

Warren: It is human nature that produces this. I write in this letter to the managers every two years and I say, the only excuse I won't take on something is that "everybody else is doing it." But, of course, "everybody else is doing it" is exactly the rationale for why people did not want to count the cost of stock options as a cost. I mean it was ridiculous. All these CEOs went to Washington and they got the Senate, I think, to vote 88 to 9 to say that stock options aren't a cost and then a few years later it became so obvious that they finally put it in so that it was a cost. It reminded me of Galileo or something. I mean, all these guys.

Charlie: Worse, way worse. The Pope behave better than Galileo, didn't he?.

Warren: Anyway, I would hope that somebody, whoever, … I'm not talking about the current successor or anybody else - that the successors down the line are probably or could have gotten very very wealthy by the time they're running Berkshire and the incremental value of wealth gets very close to zero at some point. There is a chance to use it as a different sort of model.

I don't have any problem if a system is devised that recognizes retained earnings. I've never heard anybody talk about it at the 20 boards I've been on. You know, if you and I were partners in a business and we kept retaining earnings in the business and I kept having the value to buy a portion of you out at a constant price, you would say this is idiocy. But of course, that's the way all the option systems are designed. And it's better for the CEO and consultants and, of course, usually there's some correlation between what CEOs are paid and what Boards are paid. If CEOs are getting paid at the rate they got paid 50 years ago, adapted to present dollars, sure the pay would be lower. So, it's got all these built-in things to some extent, sort of kindled ...

Charlie: No Berkshire director is in it for the money.

Warren: Well, they are. They own a lot of stock and they bought it in the market just like us.

Charlie: Yeah, it's a very old-fashioned system.

Warren: I looked at one company the other day and seven of the directors had never bought a share of stock with their own money. Now they've been given stock and seven of the directors had never actually bought a share of stock and there they are making decisions on who should be CEO and how they should be paid and all that sort of thing. But they've never felt like shelling out a dollar themselves. They've been given a lot of stock. We're dealing with human nature here, folks, and what you want is to have a system that works well, in spite of how human nature is going to drive it. We've done awfully well in this country in that respect. American business, overall, has done very very well for the Americans generally. But not every aspect of it is exactly what you want to teach your kids.

OK, Gregg.

WIDENING OF THE PANAMA CANAL AND IT'S IMPACT ON BNSF

Q26. Analyst, Gregg Warren: Warren, between 2010 and 2015 intermodal rail traffic enjoyed double digit rates of revenue growth, as shorter-haul freight converted from truck to rail. During the past year or so, though, cheaper diesel prices and more readily available truckload capacity had made trucking more competitive, leading to a decline in intermodal rail traffic. While car load growth is expected to be solid longer term helping to offset weakness in other segments like coal, what impact do you expect the widening of the Panama Canal, which was completed last year, to have on the West Coast ports shipments

that BNSF has traditionally carried through the exchange points for the eastern U.S. railroads as shippers elect to have goods unloaded at ports in the Gulf of Mexico or the Eastern Seaboard? And while loss of volumes is never a good thing, could there be a small tradeoff here as the bottleneck in Chicago (where most of the West's cargo is handed off) ease a bit over time as some of the current traffic gets rerouted?

Warren: Well. Yeah. Sure. Chicago has got lots of problems and it's going to continue for a while. I mean that requires a big solution. When you think of how the railroads developed, Chicago was the center. And you laid the rails and there were a whole bunch of different railroads, a hundred years ago. And city grows up around them and everything. So Chicago can be a huge problem.

But getting to intermodal, I think intermodal will do very well but you are correct that car loadings actually hit a peak in 2006. So here we are 11 years later and the investment of the five big class one railroads – four of the biggest - if you look at their investment beyond depreciation, it's tens and tens of billions of dollars and we're carrying less freight, in aggregate, than we were in 2006. And coal will continue to decrease.

It's a good business and it has big advantages over truck in many respects. Truck gets much more of a free ride in terms of the fact that their right of way, which is the highway system, is subsidized to a much greater degree beyond the gas tax, you know, than the railroad industry. But it has not been a growth business in physical volume to any great degree. I think it's unlikely to be. I think it's likely to be a good business. I think we've got a great territory. I like the West better than the East. And, as you mentioned, there will be some intermodal traffic that gets diverted to eastern ports perhaps. Overall, we've got a terrific system in that respect and we will do well. It would be more fun if we had something where you could expect aggregate car loadings to increase two or three or four percent a year. But I don't think that's going to happen. I do think our fundamental position is terrific. However I think we will earn decent returns on capital. But I think that's the limit of it.

Charlie?

Charlie: Nothing to add.

Warren: Okay, Station 9.

CAPITAL ALLOCATION MISTAKES

Q27. Audience, Station 9: I am Shankarananda from Gurnee, Illinois. Thank you for doing everything you do for us. I have a question. The two of you have largely avoided capital allocation mistakes by bouncing ideas off of one another. Will this continue long into Berkshire's future? I'm interested in both at headquarters and at subsidiaries.

Charlie: It can't continue very long. [laughter].

Warren: Don't get defeatist, Charlie. Any successor that's put in at Berkshire, capital allocation abilities and proven capital allocation abilities are certain to be uppermost in board's minds or, in the current case, in terms of my recommendation or Charlie's recommendation for what happens after we're not around them. Capital allocation is incredibly important at Berkshire. Right now we have $280 or $290 billion whatever it may be of shareholders equity.

If you take the next decade alone (nobody can make accurate predictions on this) but in the next 10 years if you just take ... - and depreciation, right now is another $7 billion a year something on that order - the next manager in the decade is going to have to allocate, may be, $400 billion or something like that may be more. And it's more than has already been put in and so ten years from now Berkshire will be an aggregation of businesses where more money has been put in in that decade than everything that took place ahead of time. So you need a very sensible capital allocator in the job of being CEO of Berkshire and we will have one.

It would be a terrible mistake to have someone in this job where really capital allocation might not even be their main talent. That probably should be very close to their main talent. And of course we have an advantage at Berkshire in that we do know how important that is. And there is that focus on it. And in a great many companies people get to the top through ability and sales, sometimes. They come from the legal side, sometimes - all kinds of different sides. And then they have capital allocation sort of on their hands. Now they may have established strategic thinking divisions that they may listen to investment bankers everything. But they better be able to do it themselves. And if they come from a different background or haven't done it, it's a little bit - as I put in one on my letters - I think it's like getting to Carnegie Hall playing the violin and then you walk out on the stage and they hand you a piano. I mean it is something that Berkshire would not do well if somebody was put in who had a lot of skills in other areas but really did not have an ability of capital allocation. I've talked about it as being something I call a money mind. People are going to have 120 IQ or 140 IQ or whatever it may be, very similar scoring abilities in terms of intelligence tests and some of them may have minds that are good at one kind of thing and some of another. And I've known very bright people that do not have money minds and they can make very unintelligent decisions. They can do all kinds of other things that most mortals can't do. But it just doesn't ... it isn't the way their wiring works. And I've known other people that really would not do that brilliantly. They'll do fine but on an S.A.T. test or something like that but they've never made a dumb money decision in their life and Charlie, I'm sure, has seen the same thing. So we do want somebody - and hopefully they've got a lot of talent - but we certainly do not want somebody if they lack a money mind.

Charlie?

Charlie: Well, it is also the option of buying in stock, which isn't like it's some hopeless problem. One way or another something intelligent will be done.

Warren: And a money mind who will recognize when it makes sense to buy in stock and when it doesn't. And in fact this is a pretty good test, for some people, in terms of managements, how they think about something like buying in stock; because it's not a very complicated equation, if you think straight about that sort of a subject. But some people think that way and some don't and they'll probably be miles better at something else. But they say some very silly things when you get to something that seems so clear as whether, say, buying in stock makes sense.

Anything further, Charlie?

Charlie: No.

OK, Carol?

HEDGE FUND COMPENSATION: 2-AND-20

Q28. Journalist, Carol Loomis: This question comes from Steve Haverstraw of Connecticut. Warren, you've made it very clear in your annual letter that you think the hedge fund compensation scheme of 2 and 20 generally does not work well for the fund's investors.

And in the past you have questioned whether investors should pay "financial helpers" as much as they can. But financial helpers can create tremendous value for those they help. Take Charlie Munger, for instance. In nearly every annual letter and on the movie this morning you describe how valuable Charlie's advice and counsel has been to you and, in turn, to the incredible rise in Berkshire's value of over time. Given that, would you be willing to pay the industry standard "financial helper" fee of 1 percent on assets to Charlie or would you perhaps even consider 2 and 20 for him? What is your judgment about this matter?

Warren: Well I've said in the annual report that I've known maybe a dozen people in my life - and I said there are undoubtedly hundreds or may be thousands out there. But I've said that I've known personally a dozen where I would have predicted or did predict (and there are a number of those 12 cases); I did predict that the person involved would do better than average in investing over a long period of time. And obviously Charlie is one of those people. So will I pay him? Sure. But will I take financial advisors as the group and pay them 1 percent with the idea that they would deliver results to me that were better than the S&P 500 by 1 percent and thereby leave me breaking even against what I could have done on my own? You know there are very few. So, it's just not a good question to ask whetehr you know, I'll pay Charlie 1 percent. That's like asking whether I'd pay Babe Ruth $100,000, or whatever it was, to come over from the Red Sox to the Yankees. I mean sure. But there weren't very many people I would have paid a $100,000 to somewhere in 1919 or whatever it was, to come over to the Yankees. So, it's a fascinating situation because the problem isn't that the advisers are going to do some terrible. It's just that you have an option available that doesn't cost you anything that is going to do better than they are in aggregate. And it's an interesting question.

If you hire an obstetrician, assuming you need one, they're going to do a better job of delivering the baby than if the spouse comes in to do it, or if they just pick somebody up off the street. And if you if you go to a dentist, if you hire a plumber and all of the professions, there is value added by the professionals as a group compared to doing it yourself or just randomly picking laymen. In the investment world it isn't true. I mean, the active group, the people that are professionals in aggregate are not, cannot, do better than the aggregate of the people who sit just sit tight. And if you say "well in the active group there's some person that's terrific," I will agree with you. But the passive people can't all pick that person and they don't know how to identify him.

Charlie: It's even worse than that. The expert who is really good, when he gets more and more money, he suffers just terrible performance problems.

Warren: Yeah.

Charlie: So, you'll find the person who has a long career of 2 and 20 and if you analyze it, net all of the people who have lost money, because some of the early people would have had good record but more money comes in later and they lose it. So, the investing world is a morass of wrong incentives, crazy reporting and, I would say, a fair amount of delusion.

Warren: Yeah if you asked me whether those 12 people I picked would do better than the S&P 500 working with a $100 billion, I would answer that probably none of them would. I mean that would not be their prospective performance. But when I was talking of them - when I was referencing them - and when they actually work in practice they dealt generally with pretty moderate sums and as the sums grew, their relative advantage diminished. I mean it's so obvious from history that (the example I used in the report)

I mean the guy who made the bet with me and incidentally all kinds of people didn't make the bet with me because they knew better than to make the bet with me. And then there were hundreds, at least a couple of hundred underlying hedge funds. These guys were incentivized to do well. The fund-of-funds manager was inventivized to pick the best ones they could pick. The guy who made the bet with me was incentivized to pick the best fund of funds you know and tons of money. And just with those five funds a lot of money went to pay managers for what was subnormal performance over a long period of time. And it can't be anything but that.

It's an interesting, you know, it's an interesting profession when you have tens of thousands or hundreds of thousands of people who are compensated based on selling something that in aggregate can't be true – superior performance. But it will continue and the best sales people will tend to attract the most money. And because it's such a big game people will make huge sums of money, you know, far beyond what they're going to make in medicine or you name it, you know, repairing the country's infrastructure. I mean the big money, the huge money, is in selling people the idea that you can do something magical for them. And if you have a billion dollar fund, you know, and get 2 percent of it for terrible performance, that's $20 million. In any other field, it will just blow your mind. But people get so used to it. In the field of investment it just sort of passes along and $10 billion, I mean $200 million fees. We've got two guys in the office that are managing $11 billion. No they're not. I'm sorry. Yeah they're managing $20 billion. You know between the two of them, $21 billion may be. We pay them a million dollars a year plus the amount by which they beat the S&P. They have to actually do something to get contingent compensation which is much more reasonable than the 20 percent. But how many hedge fund managers in the last 40 years have said "I only want to get paid if I do something for you.

Unless I actually deliver something beyond what you can get yourself, I don't want to get paid." It just doesn't happen. And you know it gets back to that line that I've used: when I asked the guy "how can you in good conscience charge 2 and 20?" And he said "because I can't get 3 and 30." [laughter].

Anymore, Charlie? Or we used up our…

Charlie: I think, you've beaten up on them enough.

Warren: Yeah. Well, Jonathan.

PRECISION CASTPARTS' UPDATE

Q29. Analyst, Jonathan Brandt: Precision Castparts represents the second largest acquisition Berkshire has ever made. There wasn't much qualitative or quantitative information about it in the 2016 annual. Would you be willing to update us here with how it is doing currently, what excites you about its prospects and what worries you most about it? I'm also curious if there were any meaningful purchase price adjustments beyond intangible amortization that negatively impacted Precision's earnings in 2016 as was the case with Van Tyle in 2015. And finally are there any opportunities in sight for bolt-on acquisitions?

Warren: Yeah we've actually made acquisitions and we will make more that fit because we've got an extraordinary manager and we've got a terrific position in the aircraft field. So, that will be the chance for sensible acquisitions and we've already made two anyway. And we will make more over time. The amortization of intangibles is the only big purchase price adjustment; that's something over $400 million a year non-deductible. In my mind that's $400 million and some of earnings. I do not regard the economic goodwill of Precision Castparts being diminished at that rate annually. And I've explained that in some degree.

As a very long-term business, you can worry about 3D printing. I don't think you have to worry about aircrafts being manufactured. But aircraft deliveries can be substantially altered in relation to any given backlog in most cases. So the deliveries can be fairly volatile. But I don't think the long-term demand is anything I worry about. The question is whether anybody can do it better or cheaper or, like I say, whether 3D printing, at least, takes away part of the field in some respects.

Overall, I would tell you, I feel very good about Precision Castparts. It is a very long-term business. We have contracts that run for a very long time and, like I say, the initiation of a new plant may be delayed or something of that sort. But if you take a look at the engine that is in the other adjoining room here in our exhibition hall, you would - if you were putting that engine together with a 20- or 25-year life or whatever it may have, carrying hundreds of people - you would care very much about your supplier and you'd care not only about the quality - which would be absolutely ... [necessary] ... you'd care about the work being done. But you would also, if you were an engine manufacturer or an aircraft manufacturer further down the line, you would care very much about the reliability of delivery on something, because you do not want a plane or an engine that is 99 percent complete while somebody is dealing with the problem of faulty parts or anything else that would delay delivery. So reliability is incredibly important. I don't think anybody has a reputation better than Mark Donegan and the company for delivery. So, I love the fact that we bought Precision Castparts.

Charlie?

Charlie: Yeah. Well, what is interesting about it too is that it is a very good business purchased at a fair price. But this is no screaming bargain like the old days. With quality businesses you pay up now a lot more now than we used to.

Warren: Yeah that's absolutely true. You don't get a bargain price. The $400 plus million incidentally goes on for quite a while too. We'll explain it in the report, just as we always explain, that the depreciation charge of a railroad would not be adequate. I mean it's the way accounting works. I don't even want to tell you about this one but starting on the first of next year, accounting is going to become sort of a nightmare in terms of Berkshire and other companies because they're going to have us mark our equities to market just like we were a Wall Street trading firm or something. And those changes in the value of Coca-Cola or American Express or anything else are going to run through the income account every quarter. In fact, they run through it every day on this. So, that really will get confusing now. It's our job to explain things so that you aren't confused when we report GAAP earnings. But GAAP earnings as reported will become even more meaningless looking only at the bottom line than they are now.

Charlie: That was not necessarily a good idea.

Warren: I think it's a terrible idea. But we'll deal with it. I mean it's my job to explain to what extent GAAP accounting is useful to you in evaluating Berkshire and the times when it actually distorts things. Accounting is not supposed to describe value. On the other hand, it's a terribly useful tool if understood, in order to estimate value if you're analyzing businesses. And so, in a certain way, you can't blame the auditing profession for doing what they think is their job which is not to present value although by using these market values …

Charlie: But you can blame the auditing profession for that one. That was really stupid. [laughter].

Warren: Yeah. I agree with that, actually. But we will do our best to give you ... - we are always going to give you the audited figures and then we're going to explain their shortcomings in either direction and what you should use and what you probably should ignore in looking at those numbers and using them to come to a judgment as to the value of your holdings. I'll explain it to you the same way I would explain it to my sisters or anybody else.

We want you to understand what you own and we try to cover the details that are really important in that respect. I mean there's a million things you can talk about that are just of minor importance when you're talking about a $400 billion market value. But there are other things that, if Charlie and I were talking about a company, they would be the figures and the interpretations or anything that we would regard as important in, sort of, coming to an estimate of the value of the business.

You can't knock the media; I mean they've only got a few paragraphs to describe the earnings of Berkshire every quarter. But if they simply look at bottom line numbers, what can be silly this year will become absolutely ludicrous next year because of the new rule that comes into effect for 2018.

OK, Station 10.

DUPLICATING BUFFETT'S SUCCESS

Q30. Audience, Station 10: Hello, Warren. This is a question from China. I am James Chan, a pension fund manager from China, Shanghai. My question is quite simple. What is the probability of duplicating your creative investment track record in China's stock

market in the next decade or two in terms of investment per se? That's all. And I thank my friends who came from Foogo Fund Management House for guiding me to write this question. Thank you.

Warren: Charlie, you're the expert on China. [laughter].

Charlie: It's like determining the order of presidency between a louse and a flea. I do think that the Chinese stock market is cheaper than the American market. And I do think China has a bright future. And I also think that there will be growing pains, of course.

We have this opportunistic way of going through life. We don't have any particular rules about which market we are in or anything like that.

Warren: Well, Charlie has delivered the headline anyway now. Munger prediction: China market will outperform the U.S.

And I've just been informed it's 12:15. So I apologize, if you're hungry, for holding you over for 15 minutes so we'll reconvene around 1:15 and I'll see you then. Thanks.

… Recess …

Questions and Answers: Part 2

"I mean, the last thing we'll like to do is own something at 100 times earnings where the earnings can't grow."
Warren Buffett

"...it's hard to find people young, ambitious, very smart that don't put themselves first."
Warren Buffett

"We don't want to go back to subsistence farming. I had a week of that when I was young on a Western Nebraska farm and I hated it."
Charlie Munger

Warren: OK. We're back for action. And we'll go right to Becky.

3G INVESTMENT STRATEGY

Q31. Journalist, Becky Quick: Alright. This question comes from Anne Newman and she says she is a shareholder of Class B stock. And her question is: the primary investment strategy of 3G Capital is extreme cost cutting after the purchase of a company. This typically includes the elimination of thousands of jobs. With the current U.S. President focusing on retention of U.S. jobs, will Berkshire Hathaway still consider future investments in 3G Capital if those investments result in the purchase of U.S. companies and the elimination of more U.S. jobs?

Warren: Essentially 3G management (and I've watched them very close at Kraft Heinz) is basically ... they believe in having a company as productive as possible and, of course, the gains in this world for the people in this room, people in Omaha and people throughout America have come through gains in productivity. If there had been no change in productivity, we would have been living the same life as people lived in 1776. Now the people, the 3G people, do it very fast and they're very good at making a business productive with fewer people than operated before. But we've been doing that in every industry whether it's steel or cars or you name it and that's why we live as well as we do.

We prefer at Berkshire - I wrote about this a year ago - we prefer to buy companies that are already run efficiently because frankly we don't enjoy the process at all of getting more productive. I mean it's not pleasant but it is what has enabled the country to progress and nobody has figured out a way to double people's consumption per capita without, in some way, improving productivity per capita. It's a good question whether it's smart overall, if you think you're going to suffer politically because political consequences do hit businesses. So I don't know if I can answer the question categorically. But I can tell you that they not only focus on productivity, and do it in a very intelligent way, but they also focus to a terrific degree on product improvement, innovation, and all of the other things that you want a management to focus on. And I hope that at the lunchtime if you had the Kraft Heinz cheesecake you'll agree with me that product improvement and innovation is just as much a part of the 3G playbook as productivity.

Personally, we have been through the process of buying into a textile business that employed a couple of thousand people and went out of business over a period of time or a department store business that was headed for oblivion and it is just not as much fun to be in a business that cuts jobs rather than one that adds jobs. So, Charlie and I would probably forgo, personally, having Berkshire directly buy businesses where the main benefits would come from increasing productivity by actually having fewer workers. But I think it's pro social to think in terms of improving productivity and I think the people of 3G do a very good job at that.

Charlie?

Charlie: Well, I agree. I don't see anything wrong with increasing productivity. On the other hand, there's a lot of counterproductive publicity to doing it. Just because you're right doesn't mean you should always do it.

Warren: Yeah I would agree with that.

Jay?

SHARE REPURCHASE

Q32. Analyst, Jay Gelb: Berkshire's cash and Treasury bill holdings are approaching $100 billion. Warren, a

year ago you said Berkshire might increase its minimum valuation for share buybacks above 1.2 times book value, if this occurred. What are your latest thoughts on raising the share repurchase threshold?

Warren: When the time comes - and it could come reasonably soon, even while I'm around. We really don't think we can get the money out, in a reasonable period of time, into things we like. We have to reexamine what we do with those funds that we don't think can be deployed well. And at that time we will make a decision and it might include both but it could be repurchases, it could be dividends. There are different inferences that people draw from a dividend policy than from a repurchase policy in terms of the expectations that you won't cut a dividend and that sort of thing. So you have to factor all that in. But if we really felt that we had cash that was unlikely to be used (excess cash) in a reasonable period of time and we thought repurchases at a price that was still attractive to continuing shareholders was feasible in a substantial sum, that could make a lot of sense. At the moment, we're still optimistic enough about deploying the capital that we wouldn't be inclined to move to a price much closer where there's only a narrow spread between an intrinsic value and the repurchase price. But at a point the burden of proof is definitely on us. I mean, the last thing we'll like to do is own something at 100 times earnings where the earnings can't grow. As you point out, we've got almost $100 billion, $90+ billion invested in a business, we will call it a business, where we're paying almost 100 times earnings and it's kind of a lousy business.

Charlie: It's more if it is after-tax earnings.

Warren: So, you know, we don't like that and we shouldn't use your money that way for a long period of time. And then the question is, are we going to be able to deploy it? I would say that history is on our side. But it will be more fun if the phone would ring instead of just relying on history books.

I am sure that sometime in the next 10 years (and it could be next week or it could be 9 years from now), there would be markets in which we can do intelligent things on a big scale. But it would be no fun if that happens to be nine years off - and I don't think it will be - but just based on how humans behave, how governments behave, and how the world behaves. But, like I say, at a point, the burden of proof really shifts to us big time. And there's no way I can come back here three years from now and tell you that we hold a $150 billion or so in cash or more and we think we're doing something brilliant by doing it.

Charlie?

Charlie: Well I agree with you. The answer is "may be." [laughter].

Warren: He does have a tendency to elaborate.

Station 11.

BUSINESS PRACTICES AT CTB INC.

Q33. Audience, Station 11: Thank you Mr. Buffett and Mr. Munger. I am Anil Narayan from Short Hills, New Jersey and New Delhi, India. This is my 18th time to this wonderful event and I profoundly thank you for your extraordinary wisdom, generosity and time. As I'm involved with sustainable investments that also do not directly harm animals, I would appreciate your perspective, if any, on the practices of your CTB

subsidiary which is somewhat involved in pig, poultry and egg production - somewhat indirectly related, as you shared your concern on nuclear war extensively at the last annual meeting. I would love to pick your brain on Albert Schweitzer's Nobel Peace Prize acceptance speech shortly after the first nuclear bombs were detonated, that compassion can only attain its full breadth and depth if it is not limited to humans only. Thank you.

Warren: Well, that's a pretty broad question. I would say on your first point we have a subsidiary, CTB run by Vic Mancinelli and I sit down with him once a year and he is a terrific manager, one of our very best. You don't hear much about him. And they do make the equipment for poultry growers. I can't answer your question specifically but I would be glad to have you get in contact with Vic directly because I know that question you raise is a major factor in what they do. I mean they they do care about how the equipment is used in terms of poultry and egg production. And, as you know, a number of the largest purchasers and the largest producers are also in the same camp. I can't tell you enough about it directly that I can give you a specific answer but I can certainly put you in touch with Vic. And I think you would find him extremely well informed and doing some very good things in the area that you're talking about.

In terms of the nuclear weapon question, I'm very pessimistic on weapons of mass destruction, generally, although I don't think that nuclear probably is quite as likely as either biological, (primarily biological) or, maybe, cyber. I don't know that much about cyber but I do think that's the number one problem of mankind. But I don't think I can say anything particularly constructive on it now.

Charlie?

Charlie: I don't think we mind killing chickens. [laughter]. And I do think we are against nuclear war. So... [laughter and applause].

Warren: We are not actually a poultry producer but they use our equipment and that equipment has been changed substantially in the last 10 or 15 years. But again, I'm just not that good on the specifics that I can give them to you but I can certainly put you in touch with Vic.

Andrew?

TED WESCHLER AND TODD COMBS

Q34. Journalist, Andrew Ross Sorkin: Warren, since Todd and Ted joined Berkshire the market cap the company has doubled and cash on hand is now nearly $100 billion. It doesn't look like Todd and Ted have been allocated new capital on the same relative basis. Why?

Warren: Well, actually I would say they have been. I think we started out with $2 billion. I could be wrong but my memory was $2 billion with Todd when he came with us. So there have been substantial additions and, of course, their own capital is growing just because, you'd say in a sense, they retained their own earnings. They are managing a proportion of Berkshire's capital or also measured by marketable securities. I think they are managing a proportion that's pretty similar or maybe even a little higher than when each one of them entered, and Ted entered a year or two after Todd. I think they would agree that it's tougher to run $10 billion than it is to run one or two billion. I mean your expectable returns go down as you get into larger sums.

The decision to bring them on has been terrific. I mean they have done a good job of managing marketable securities. They made more money than I would have made with that same - what it is now $20 billion, but originally it was two billion. And they've been a terrific help in a variety of ways beyond just money management. So, that decision has been a very very good decision. They are smart. They have money minds. They are good specifically at investment management. They are absolutely first class human beings and they really fit that Berkshire. Charlie gets credit for Todd. He met Charlie first and I'll claim credit for Ted and I think we both feel very good about the decisions.

Charlie?

Charlie: Well, I think the shareholders are very lucky to have them because they both think like shareholders.

Warren: Totally.

Charlie: It came up that way and that is not the normal way that Edwards employees think. It's a pretense that everybody takes on but the reality is different. And these people really deeply think like shareholders and they're young and smart and constructive. So we're all very lucky to have them around.

Warren: Yeah their mindset is 100 percent what can I do for Berkshire not what can Berkshire do for me. And, believe me, you can spot that over time with people. And on top of that they're very talented. But it's hard to find people young, ambitious, very smart that don't put themselves first. And I would say again, from experience we've had, that they do not put themselves first. They put Berkshire first. And, believe me, I can spot it when people are extreme in one direction or another; may be I'm not so good around the middle. But you couldn't have two better people in those positions. But you would say well "why don't you give them another $30 billion each or something?" I don't think that would improve their lives or their performance. They may be handling more as they go along. But the truth is I've got more assigned to me than I can handle at the present time as proven by the fact that we've got this $90 billion plus around. I think there are reasonable prospects for using it. But if you told me I had to put it to work today, I would not like the prospect.

Charlie?

Charlie: Well I certainly agree with that. It's a lot harder now, was at times in the past.

Gregg?

PURCHASING CLASS A SHARES FROM EXISTING SHAREHOLDERS

Q35. Analyst, Gregg Warren: Warren, plans for your ownership stake which is heavily concentrated in Class A shares are fairly well known, with the bulk of the stock going to the Bill and Melinda Gates Foundation and four different family charities over time. Your annual pledges to these different charities involve the conversion of Class A shares which hold significantly greater voting rights to the Class B shares. As such the voting control held by your estate will diminish over time with the whole of layer of super voting shares being eliminated in the process. While the voting

influence of Class **B** shareholders are expected to increase over time, it will not be large enough to have a big influence on Berkshire's affairs. With that in mind, and recognizing the great importance of having Berkshire buyback and retire Class **A** shares in the long run, I was just wondering if the firm has compiled the pipeline of potential future sellers from the ranks of the company's existing shareholders. Given the limited amount of liquidity for the shares privately negotiated transactions with these sellers, like the one you negotiated in December 2012, would end up being in the best interests of both parties.

Warren: Well, again it would depend on the price of Berkshire. So, in terms of what I give away annually, the last two years it's been about $2.8 billion per year. That's one day's trading in an apple. The amount of giving away in terms of Berkshire's market cap, you're down to seven tenths of one percent of the market cap. So it's not a big market factor and it really won't be that illiquid. I know a few big holders that might have eight or ten thousand shares of A but the market can handle it.

Now, when we bought that block of, I think, 12,000 shares of A, we bought it because we thought it would increase the intrinsic business value of Berkshire by a significant amount. We paid the seller what the market was at the time and we are open to that up to 120 percent. And who knows if it came along at the time and it was 124 percent or something. It was a very large block and the directors decided that it was OK. It still was a significant discount; we might very well buy it. But in terms of the orderly flow of the market or anything like that there will be no problems just as there haven't been, you know, when I've given away - I do it every July - when I've given away the last two years.

Some of the foundations may keep it for a while but they have to spend what I give them. And they may build up a position in B, you know, of a fairly significant dollar amount but they're going to sell it. And it is true that for a period after I die, there will be a lot of votes still in the estate and later in the trust but that will get reduced over time. I see no problem with our capitalization over time.

I like the idea of a fair number of votes being concentrated with people that believe in the culture strongly and would not be thinking about whether they get a 20 percent jump in the stock if somebody came along with some particular plan. But, eventually, that's going to get diminished; it continues to get diminished. I think there's a very good market in Berkshire shares and if we can buy them at a discount from intrinsic business value and somebody offers us some - a big piece – and the stock may be selling at 122 percent or 124 percent, you know I would pick up the phone and call the directors and see if they didn't want to make a change. We did it once before and if it made sense, I'm sure they'd say yes if it didn't make sense I'm sure they'd say no. So, I don't think we have any problem in terms of blocks of stock or anything. I don't think the owner will have a problem selling it and I don't think we have a problem in terms of evaluating the desirability of repurchasing it.

Charlie?

Charlie: Nothing to add.

Okay, Station 1.

Q36. Audience, Station 1: Hello my name is Erin Bayer and I was born and raised in Pasadena California and I currently live in New York City. It's been a dream of

mine to come here today. I've been a proud shareholder for almost 20 years. I asked my dad first stock for Christmas when I was 15 and I kept thinking that if I had the opportunity to ask you a question today, that I should make it one that would change my life. Well, that question is: do you know any eligible bachelors living in the New York City area? [laughter].

Warren: You certainly have the approach toward life that Charlie and I would have.

BANK OF AMERICA PREFERRED STOCKS

Erin: But the question that might make my Monday, back in the office: Back in 2011 you purchased Bank of America preferred stock with a warrant. You have the opportunity at a later date to exercise and convert those into common shares. When you're looking at evaluating that decision to exercise that position which would increase all of our Berkshire holdings or the value of Berkshire holdings, what you are going to consider when you're looking at that.

Warren: Well, if the price of the stock is above $7 a share, which seems quite likely, whether we were going to keep it or not it would still make sense for us to exercise the warrant shortly before it expired because it would be a valuable warrant but it's only a valuable warrant if it's converted or if it is exercised and exchanged into common and that warrant does expire. As I put it in the annual report, our income from the investment would increase if the Bank of America ever got to where it was paying 11 cents quarterly.

We get $300 million a year off the preferred. For us to use the preferred as payment in the exercise of the warrant, we would need and we would want to feel we were getting more than $300 million a year and that would take 11 cents quarterly. They may or may not get to where they paid that amount before the warrant expires in 2021. If it does get there, we will exercise the warrant and then instead of owning the $5 billion of preferred and the warrant we'll have 700 plus million shares of common then that becomes a separate decision. Do we want to keep the 700 million shares of common? If it were to happen today I would definitely want to keep the stock. Now who knows what other alternatives may be available in 2021. But as of today, if our warrants were expiring tomorrow we would use the preferred to buy 700 million plus shares of common and we would keep the common.

If they get to 11 cents quarterly dividend we'll convert it and we'll very likely keep the common. And when we get to 2021, if the common is above $7 which I would certainly anticipate, we will exercise.

So, that's all I can tell you on that. But I certainly wish you success on your other objective. [laughter]. And I think probably the fellow will be using very good judgment too.

Okay, Charlie?

Charlie: Well, I think it's a very wise thing for a woman who owns Berkshire stocks and it's a good looking woman to put her picture up like that. [laughter].

Warren: It does give me a thought though. We might actually start selling ads in the annual report. [laughter].

That incident, that B of A purchase, it literally was true that I was sitting in the bath tub when I got the idea of checking with the B of A whether they'd be interested in that preferred. But I spent a lot of time in the bath tub since and nothing has come to me. So, clearly, I either need a new bath tub or we've got to get into a different kind of market.

Carol?

3G CAPITAL

Q37. Journalist, Carol Loomis: This is a question from Geroge Benaroya and it adds a layer to the discussion about 3G and a little bit ago. He says: "I'm a very happy long-term shareholder but this is a concern I have regarding Berkshire Hathaway's Kraft Heinz investment. This investment has done well in economic terms. The current value is $15 billion and the market value was $28 billion in 2016. But the DNA of 3G is quite different from ours. We do not make money by buying companies and firing people. 3G fired 2,500 employees at Kraft Heinz. That is what private equity firms do. But we are not a private equity firm. Our values have worked for us for over 50 years. There is a risk that if 3G continues to deviate from our principles, they will eventually harm both our value and our values. How do we prevent that from happening?"

Warren: Well, it's interesting. I mentioned earlier that it was very gradual but it would have been probably a better decision: we fired 2,000 people over time. Some retired and left and all of that. But at the textile operation, you know it didn't work. And at Hochschild-Kohn, the successor, fortunately, sold it to somebody else. But eventually they closed up the department stores because department stores – at least, that particular one, and a good many, actually, including our competitors in Baltimore - could not make it work. Wal-Mart came along with something and now Amazon is coming along with something that changed the way people bought things.

We mentioned our poultry, CTB, which sells a lot of different farm equipment. The farm equipment often that CTB develops - the idea is that it's more productive than what already is out there which means fewer people are employed on farms.

We had 80 percent of the American (population) working population working on farms a couple of hundred years ago. And if nobody had come up with things to make a more productive farming, we would have 80 percent of people working on farms now to feed our populace and it means that we'll be living in a far far more primitive way. So, if you look at the auto industry, it gets more productive. If you look at any industry, they are trying to get more productive.

Wal-Mart was more productive than department stores and that will continue in America. And it better continue or we won't live any better and our kids won't live any better than we do. Our kids will live better than we do because America does get more productive as it goes along and people do come up with better ways of doing things.

When Kraft Heinz finds that they can do whatever amount of business ($27 billion worth of business or something) and they can do it with fewer people, they are doing what American business has done for a couple hundred years and why we live so well. But they do it very fast. They are more than fair in terms of severance pay and all of that sort of thing. But they don't want to have two people doing the job that one can do.

I frankly don't like going through that. Having faced that, I faced that down at Dempsters in Beatrice, Nebraska and it really needed change. But the change is painful for a lot of people and I just would rather spend my days not doing that sort of thing, having had one or two experiences. But I think that it's absolutely essential to America that we become more productive because that is the only way we have more consumption per capita; that is, to have more productivity per capita.

Charlie?

Charlie: Well, you're absolutely right. We don't want to go back to subsistence farming. I had a week of that when I was young on a Western Nebraska farm and I hated it. [laughter]. And I don't miss the elevator operators who used to sit there all day in the elevator round the little crank, you know. So, on the other hand, as you said, it's terribly unpleasant for the people that have to go through it and why would we want to get into the business of doing that over and over ourselves. We did it in the past when we had to when the businesses were dying. I don't see any moral fault in 3G at all. But I do see that there is some political reaction that doesn't do anybody any good.

Warren: Milton Friedman, I think, used to talk about the time, probably apocryphal. He would talk about the huge construction project in some communist country with thousands and thousands and thousands of workers out there with shovels digging away on this major project. And then they had a few of these big earthmoving machines behind which were idle and which could have done the work in one-twentieth of the time of the workers. So, the economists suggested to the local party worker, or whoever it was, that why in the world didn't they use these machines

123

to get the job done and one-tenth or one-twentieth of the time instead of having all these workers out there with shovels. And the guy replied "well, oh yeah, but that would put the workers out of work." And Friedman said well, then why don't you give them spoons to do it instead. [laughter].

Jonathan?

BERKSHIRE'S CASH AT HAND

Q38. Analyst, Jonathan Brandt: I understand that Berkshire is much more liquid than is ideal right now with $113 billion of consolidated cash and bonds versus policyholder float of $105 billion. But I have trouble calculating how much incremental buying power Berkshire has at any point in time. You've talked about having a minimum of $20 billion in cash on a consolidated basis. But for regulatory risk controller liquidity purposes, is there some minimum amount of float beyond the $20 billion that has to be in cash, bonds, or safe preferred stocks. Or, can all but $20 billion be put into either common stocks or invested into wholly owned businesses, if you found attractive opportunities? What does the balance sheet look like if you were fully invested and where does additional debt fit into the equation, if at all?

Warren: Yeah, I wouldn't conflate the cash and the bonds. When we talk about $20 billion in cash, we could own bonds beyond that. $20 billion would be the absolute minimum. It's a practical matter. Since I've said $20 billion is a minimum, I'm not going to operate with $21 billion anymore than I'm going to see on a highway a truck sign that says maximum load 30,000 pounds or something and then drive 29,800 across it. So we won't come that close.

The answer is that we're not inclined to use debt, but obviously, if we found something that really lit our fire we might use some more debt although it is unlikely under today's circumstances. But $20 billion is an absolute minimum. You can say that because I say $20 billion is an absolute minimum, it probably wouldn't be below $24 or $25 and we could do a very very large deal if we thought it was sufficiently attractive. I mean we have not put our foot to the floor on anything for really a very long time. But if we saw something really attractive, ...

We spent $16 billion back when we were much smaller in a period of two or three weeks, probably three weeks, maybe, in the fall of 2008. And we never got to a point where it was any problem for me sleeping at night and now we obviously have a lot more money to put out.

Charlie, at what point if I called you would you say I think that's a little bit big for us today?

Charlie: I would say about $150 billion.

Warren: Well, in that case I'll call you. [laughter]. I'm a little more conservative on that than actually Charlie. But we'll both would do a very very big deal.

Charlie: We don't have to agree perfectly.

Warren: Yeah, it had to be. But if we find a really big deal that makes compelling sense...

Charlie: Now you're talking.

Warren: We're going to do it.

OK, Station 2.

JORGE PAULO LEMANN

Q39. Audience, Station 2: Hello Mr. Buffett and Mr. Munger. My name is Philippe Piccione. I'm 19 years old from Brazil. Your partnership with Jorge Paulo Lemann and his associates at 3G has been very successful taking into account great outcome of transactions such as the Kraft Heinz merger. Even though you and Jorge Paulo have different investment methods, would you and Charlie consider him to be a member of your board or even your successor?

Warren: I don't think that will happen. I think it would complicate things in terms of the board membership. But we love the idea of being their partner and I think there's a good chance that we will do more and perhaps even bigger things together. But we are probably unlikely to be doing much change in the board. Certainly, in the next few years, there will be a successor and this successor could very well be while I'm alive. But there's a very high probability that it will be somebody that's been in our company for some time. I mean the world could change in very strange ways. But that has a very very high probability.

Charlie?

Charlie: All I can say is that my back hurts when I come to these functions and I want to indicate to my fellow shareholders that they've probably got seven more good years to get out of Warren. [laughter].

Warren: Charlie is inspiring me, I've got to tell you that. We've been very very very lucky in life. And so far our luck seems to be holding.

OK, Becky.

FRUIT OF THE LOOM

Q40. Journalist, Becky Quick: This question comes from Drew Estes in Atlanta, Georgia and he asks: "Is Fruit of the Loom experiencing difficulties related to the distribution channel shift towards online and the troubles in the brick and mortar retail world? If so, do you believe the difficulties are short-term in nature?" And then Drew goes on to add, "I'm hoping millennials haven't bucked the underwear trend too."

Warren: Well he may know more about that than I do. The answer is, essentially, no so far. But anybody that doesn't think that online isn't changing retail in a big way and anybody who thinks they're are totally insulated from it is incorrect. The world is changing big time. And I could say that Fruit of the Loom really hasn't changed that much and our furniture operation which is setting a record so far. Again this year, for the shareholders weekend, you know I mentioned in the report I think we did $45 million in one week. And our furniture operations, it's hard to see any effect from online, outside of our own online operations.

We had really good same store gains. You can take, you know, Nebraska Furniture Mart or R.C. Willey whether it's in Sacramento or Reno or Boise or Salt Lake City or Jordan which in Boston has done very well on a same store basis. So we don't really see it but there were a lot of things we didn't see 10 years ago that then materialized.

One thing you may find interesting is that the furniture mart here in Omaha - which is an extraordinary operation - the online is growing very substantially. And, I may be wrong on this, but I think it's getting up to (I'd like to check this with the mart before I say it) but I think it's getting pretty close to 10 percent or so of volume. But a very significant percentage of those people still go in and pick the product up at the furniture mart. So apparently, it's the time spent entering the store or, maybe, at checkout lines or whatever it may be, I'm surprised that it gets to be that percentage. But the one thing about it is we keep looking at the figures and trying to figure out what they're telling us. So far I would not say that it's affected Fruit of the Loom in a significant manner. I would not say it's affected the furniture operation in a significant manner. But I have no illusions that 10 years from now is going to look anything like today.

If you think about it, you know, if you go back 100 years to the great department stores what did they offer? They offered incredible selection. You know if you had a big department store in Omaha you had the thousand bridal dresses and if you lived in a small town around the local guy had two or something of the sort. So the department store was the big exciting experience of variety and decent prices and convenient transportation because people took the streetcars to get there and then along came the shopping center and they took what was vertical before and they made it horizontal and they changed it into multiple ownerships but they still kept incredible variety and assortments and convenience of going to one place and accessible transportation because now the car was the method. And then we went through the discount stores and all of that. But now you've got the Internet and you've got the ultimate in terms of of of assortments and you've got people that are coming in at low prices and and the transportation is taken care of entirely.

The evolution that has taken place, the department store, is online now basically except much expanded and assortment, much more convenient, and lower prices. So, the world has evolved and it's going to keep evolving but the speed has increased dramatically. And what will happen is the brands are going to be tested in a variety of ways and they have to make decisions as to whether they try to do it online themselves or work through an Amazon or whether they try to hang on to the old methods of distribution while embracing new ones. There is a lot of questions in retail and in branding that are very interesting to watch and you'll get some surprises in the next 10 years, I can promise you that.

Charlie?

Charlie: It will certainly be unpleasant if we were in the department store business. Just think of what we avoided, Warren.

Warren: We got very lucky actually because we were in the department store business and our business was so lousy that we recognized it. If it did a little bit better, we would have hung on. We owe a tremendous gratitude to Sandy Gottesman, our director who is here in the front row, because he got us out of the business when Charlie and I and Sandy were partners in that. And something that we paid six dollars a share for, I think is worth a hundred thousand dollars a share now because we got out of the business. And if it did a somewhat better business, you know, it might be worth $10 or $12 a share now. Sometimes you get lucky. We don't miss it either. Do we, Charlie?

Charlie: No, we don't miss it.

Jay?

"I think it's a very good sign that you bought Apple. It shows either one of two things – either you've gone crazy or you're learning. I prefer the learning explanation."
Charlie Munger

"Valuation of a business is not reducible to any formula where you can actually put in the variables perfectly."
Warren Buffett

"There's nothing like personal painful experience, if you want to learn. And we certainly had our share of it."
Charlie Munger

BERKSHIRE'S INTRINSIC VALUE

Q41. Analyst, Jay Gelb: This question is on Berkshire's intrinsic value. A substantial portion of the company's value is driven by operating businesses rather than the performance of the securities portfolio. Also the values of previously acquired businesses are not marked up to their economic value including **GEICO, Mid-American** and **Burlington Northern.** Based on these factors, is book value per share still a relevant metric for valuing Berkshire?

Warren: Well, it's got some relevance but it's got a whole lot less relevance than it used to and that's why I don't want to drop the book value per share factor. But the market value tends to have more significant as the decades roll along. It's a starting point and clearly our securities aren't worth more than we're carrying them for at that time. On the other hand, you've got the kind of businesses you mentioned but we've got some small businesses that are worth ten times or so but we've also got some clunkers too.

I think the best method, of course, is just to calculate the intrinsic business value but it can't be precise. We think the probability is exceptionally high that 120 percent understates it although if it was all securities, you know 120 percent would be too high. But as the businesses evolve, as we build-in unrecognized value at the operating businesses (unrecognized for accounting purposes), I think it still has some use as being the base figure that we use.

If it were a private company and 10 of us here own it, we'll just sit down annually and calculate the businesses one by one and and use that as a base value. But that gets pretty subjective when you've got as many as we do. So, I think, the easiest thing is to use the standard we're using now, recognizing the limitations in them.

Charlie?

Charlie: Yeah, I think that equities in the insurance company offsetting shareholders equity in the company are really not worth the full market value because they're locked away in a high tech system. And so I basically like it when our marketable securities go down and our own businesses go up.

Warren: Now we're working to that end. We've been working that way for 30 years now or something like that.

Charlie: We've done a very good job too. We've replaced a lot of marketable securities with unmarketable securities that are worth a lot more.

Warren: Yeah and it's actually a more enjoyable way to operate too, beyond that.

Charlie: Yeah, we know a lot of people we wouldn't otherwise be with – good people.

Warren: OK, Station 3.

INVESTMENT IN TECH COMPANIES

Q42. Audience, Station 3: Hello.

Warren: Hi.

Audience: My name is Michael Monohan and I'm from Long Island, New York. I don't know if this question qualifies as investment advice so I've a short different question if you don't want to answer this one. Unlike the last shareholder from Zone 3 this will not be a stump speech nor a protest. One of your most well known pieces of investment advice is to buy what you know. Additionally, you said earlier one of the main criteria for buying is if you could ever understand the business. Ever since I came to my first meeting in 2011 you were not known for being a tech guy. You've said smartphones are too smart for you. You don't have a computer at your desk and you've only tweeted nine times in the last four years. [laughter].

Warren: It was either that or going to a monastery. [laughter].

Michael: Despite this you've recently been investing, looking. and talking more about tech companies. My question to you and also to Charlie to comment is what turned you from the Oracle of Omaha to the Tech Maven of Omaha?

Warren: Well, I don't think I've talked that much about tech companies but the truth is we made a large investment - I made a large investment - in IBM which has not turned out that well. We haven't lost money but in terms of the bull market we've been in it's been a significant laggard. And then fairly recently we took a large position in Apple which I do regard as more of a consumer goods company in terms of certain economic characteristics, although it has a huge tech component in terms of what that product can do or what other people might come along to do to leapfrog it in some way. But I think I'll end up being (no guarantees) 1 for 2 instead of 0 for 2 but we'll find out.

Charlie?

Warren: I make no pretense whatsoever of being on the intellectual level of some 15 year old that's got an interest in tech. I think I may have some insights into consumer behavior. I certainly can get a lot of information on consumer behavior and then try to draw inferences about what that means about what consumer behavior is likely to be in the future. But we will find out.

The one thing I'll guarantee is I'll make some mistakes on marketable securities (I made them in other areas than tech). So you will not bat a 1000 no matter what industries you try to stick with. I know insurance pretty well but I think we probably lost money on an insurance stock, perhaps once or twice over the years. So, you don't bat a thousand. But I have no real knowledge about tech in the last ... well, since I was born, actually.
Charlie?

Charlie: I think it's a very good sign that you bought Apple. It shows either one of two things – either you've gone crazy or you're learning. [laughter]. I prefer the learning explanation.

Warren: So do I, actually.

Andrew?

ARTIFICIAL INTELLIGENCE

Q43. Journalist, Andrew Ross Sorkin: Hi Warren. This one's a fun one. Thomas [Khamé?] is here. He's a 27 year old shareholder from Kentfield, California. And I should preface this question by saying that he was here

17 years ago at 10 years old, asked you a question from the audience, asking you if the Internet might hurt some of Berkshire's investments. At the time you said you wanted to see how things would play out. He's now updated the question. What do you think about the implications of artificial intelligence on Berkshire's businesses beyond autonomous driving and GEICO (which you've talked about already)? In your conversations with Bill Gates, have you thought through which other businesses will be most impacted? And do you think Berkshire's current businesses will have significantly more or less employees a decade from now as a function of artificial intelligence? We mixed a couple of questions together.

Warren: Yeah, I certainly have no special insights on artificial intelligence but I will bet a lot of things happen in that field in the next couple of decades and probably a shorter timeframe. They should lead, I would certainly think (but again I don't bring much to this party) but I would certainly think they would result in a significantly less employment in certain areas but that's good for society. It may not be good for a given business.

But let's take it to the extreme. Let's assume one person could push a button and essentially two various machines, robotics and all kinds of things turn out all of the output we have in this country. So everybody has just as much output as we have now and it's all being done by - you know, instead of 150 million people being employed – by one person; is the world better off or not? Well, certainly less hours of work per week and so on. I mean it would be a good thing but it would require enormous transformation in how people relate to each other, what they expect of government, and all kinds of things. And, of course, as a practical matter, more than one person would keep working.

But pushing the idea that way, you'd certainly think that's one of the consequences of making great progress in artificial intelligence and that's enormously prosocial. Eventually, it's enormously disruptive in other ways and it can have huge problems in terms of democracy and how it reacts to that. It's similar to the problem we have in trade where trade is beneficial to society but the people who see the benefits day by day of trade, don't see a price at Wal-Mart on socks (or whatever they're importing) that says, "you are paying X but you would pay X plus so many cents if you bought this domestically." So they are getting these small and invisible benefits and the guy that gets hurt by it - who is the roadkill of free trade - feels that very specifically and that translates into politics. It gets very uncertain as to how the world would adjust, in my view, to great increases in productivity.

Without knowing a thing about it, I think that artificial intelligence would have hugely beneficial social effect but a very unpredictable political effect, if it came and fast, which I think it could.

Charlie?

Charlie: Well, you're painting a very funny world where everybody is engaged in trade and trade is "I give you golf lessons and you dye my hair." That would be a world, ... kind of like the royal family of Kuwait or something. And I don't think it would be good for America to have everything produced by one person and the rest of us just engaged in leisure.

Warren: How about if we just got twice as productive in a short period of time so that 75 million people could do it what 150 million people are doing now.

Charlie: You'd be amazed how quickly people would react to that.

Warren: In what way?

Charlie: Favorably. That's what happened during a period when everybody remembers with such affection, back in the Eisenhower years - 5% a year or something? - people loved it. Nobody complained that they were getting air conditioning and that they didn't have it before. Nobody wanted to go back to the stinking sweating nights in the south.

Warren: If you cut everybody's hours in half that's one thing; but if you fire half the people the other half keep working - I just think it gets very unpredictable. I think we saw some of that in this election because ...

Charlie: We have adjusted to an enormous amount of it. It just came along a few percent per year.

Warren: Well, and the question then is ... I don't think it worked.

Charlie: I don't think you have to worry about coming out of 25 percent a year. I think you have to worry about that you're going to get less than 2 percent a year. That's what's worrisome.

Warren: OK, we'll move on. But it's an absolutely fascinating subject to see what happens with this. It's very

very hard to predict. If in some way, you know, we've got 36000 people, say, employed at GEICO and if you could perform all of the same functions, virtually all of the same functions, and do with five or ten thousand people and it came on quickly and the same thing was happening in a great many other areas, I don't think we've ever experienced anything quite like that and, maybe, we won't experience anything like in the future. I don't know that much about AI but …

Charlie: I don't think you have to worry about that.

Warren: Well, that's because I'm 86. [laughter].

Charlie: It's not going to come that quickly.

Okay, Gregg.

BERKSHIRE HATHAWAY ENERGY

Q44. Analyst, Gregg Warren: Warren, during the past five years Berkshire Energy's investments in solar and wind generation have been about equal with around $4.7 billion dedicated to capital projects in each segment. Based on the company's end of year capital spending forecast for 2017 through 2019, investments in wind generation are expected to be more than seven times greater than investments in solar generation in the next three years with just over $4.5 billion going into wind generation. Just wondering, how much of that future spending is tied to PacifiCorp's recently announced $3.5 billion expansion plan which is heavily weighted towards improving and expanding the subsidiaries of existing wind fleet and whether the economics for wind are that much better than solar,

given that Mid-American has also been spending heavily on wind investments? Or is this just disparity between the two segments being driven more by genuine capacity needs, which would imply that you have much more solar capacity than you need?

Warren: Yeah, we don't look at it as having more solar capacity than we need or anything like. It's really a question of what comes along. I mean the projects, they are internally generated, they are externally offered to us, and we've got a big appetite for wind or solar. We have seen - just based on those figures - we have seen more wind lately but we have no bias toward either one. I mean, if we saw $5 billion of attractive solar project we could do and didn't happen to see any wind during that period, it wouldn't slow us down from doing the $5 billion or vice versa. So, we have an appetite, a huge appetite, for projects in either area.

We're particularly well situated (I think I've explained or talked about in the past) because we pay lots of taxes and therefore - solar and wind projects all involve a tax aspect to them - we can handle those much better than many other, certainly electric utilities.

Most electric utilities really don't have that much money left over after dividends and frequently the taxes aren't that significant. At Berkshire, we pay lots of taxes and we've got lots of money. So, it's really just a question of doing the math on the deals as they come along.

We've been very fortunate in Iowa in finding lots of projects that made sense and as a result we've got a much lower price for electricity than our main competitor in the state. We've got a lower price than in any states that touch us. We've told the people of Iowa they won't have a price increase for many

many many years. We guaranteed that. So it's worked out extremely well.

But if somebody walks in with a solar project tomorrow and it takes a billion dollars or it takes $3 billion, we are ready to do it. The more the better. There's no specific preference between the two. Obviously, it depends where you are in the country. Iowa is terrific for wind and obviously California is terrific for sun and there are geographical advantages to one or the other. But from our standpoint we can do them in any place and we will do them any place.

Okay, Station 4.

AMAZON AND JEFF BEZOS

Q45. Audience, Station 4: Hi, my name is Joey and I'm an MBA candidate at Wharton. Thank you for having us. Amazon has been hugely disruptive due to the brilliance of Jeff Bezos whom Charlie earlier called the business mind of our generation. What is your current outlook on Amazon and why hasn't Berkshire bought in?

Warren: Well, because I was too dumb to realize what was going to happen, even though I admired Jeff. I've admired him for a long long time and watched what he was doing. But I did not think that he could succeed on the scale he has. I certainly didn't even think about the possibility of doing anything with Amazon Web Services or the Cloud.

If you had asked me the chances that while he was building up the retail operation, that he would also be doing something that was disrupting the tech industry, that would have been a very very long shot for me. I underestimated, I really underestimated the brilliance of the execution.

It's one thing to dream about doing this stuff online but it takes a lot of ability and - you can read his 1997 annual report - he laid out a road map and he's done it and done it in spades.

If you haven't seen his interview on Charlie Rose three or four months ago (https://charlierose.com/) go to it and listen to it because you'll learn a lot. At least, It always looked expensive and I really never thought that he would be where he is today. I thought he was really brilliant. But I did not think he would be where he is today when I looked at it 3, 5, 8, or 12 years ago, whatever it may have been. Charlie, how did you miss it? [laughter].

Charlie: It was easy. What he has done there was very difficult and it was not at all obvious that it was all going to work as well as it did. I don't feel any regret about missing out on the achievements of Amazon. But other things were easier and I think we screwed up a little.

Warren: We won't pursue that line.

Charlie: Well, I meant Google.

Warren: We missed a lot of things.

Charlie: Yes.

Warren: We've missed a lot of things.

Charlie: And we'll keep doing it. [laughter]. Luckily we didn't miss everything. That's our secret. We don't miss them all. [laughter].

Warren: OK, we'd better move on. [applause]. He may start getting specific.

Carol?

SHARE REPURCHASE

Q46. Journalist, Carol Loomis: The creator of this question, Jim Kiefer of Atlanta has even higher expectations for Warren's longevity than Charlie does. Mr. Buffett, we all hope you win the record as mankind's oldest living person. But at some point you and Charlie will go and Berskhire stock may then come under selling pressure. My question is if Berkshire stock falls through a price where share repurchase is attractive, can we count on the board and top management to repurchase shares? I ask this question both because of past comments you've made about not wanting to take advantage of shareholders and because some of the passages in the Owner's Manual lead me to believe this might be an instance when the board does not choose to repurchase shares. Can you clarify what course of action we might expect about repurchases in the circumstances I have outlined?

Warren: As far as I'm concerned they are not taking advantage of shareholders if they buy the stock when it is undervalued. That's the only way they should buy it. But in doing so, there were a few cases, back when Charlie and I were much younger, where there were very aggressive repurchases or the equivalent of purchases by people (and the repurchases incidentally made a lot more sense than they do now) but they were done by people who either for various techniques tried to depress the shares.

If you're trying to encourage your partners to sell out at a depressed price by various techniques including misinformation (and there are other techniques), I think that's reprehensible. Our board won't do that.

I'll take exception to the first part of it but I'll still answer the second. I think the stock is more likely to go up. If I die tonight the stock will go up tomorrow. There'll be speculation about breakups and all that sort of thing. It would be a good Wall Street story – "this guy that obstructed breaking up something where the sum of the parts might sell for more than the whole." That probably would be worth less than the whole but it might sell temporarily for more than the whole and it will get happen. So I would bet in that direction. But if for some reason it went down to a level that's attractive, I don't think the board is doing anything in the least reprehensible by buying the stock at that point that there is no false information, nothing. Their buying means that the seller would get a somewhat better price. If there are a lot of sellers, they'll get a mildly better price than if they weren't buying; and the continuing stockholders would benefit.

I think it's obvious what they would do and I would think it's obvious that it's pro shareholder to do it. And I think they would engage in pro shareholder acts as far as the eye can see. I mean we've got that sort of Board.

Charlie?

Charlie: Well, I think you or I might suddenly get very stupid very quickly but I don't think our Board is going to have that problem. [laughter].

Warren: Well, I want to think about that one.

OK, Jonathan?

ACCOUNTING FOR OPTIONS GRANTS

Q47. Analyst, Jonathan Brandt: Warren, in the past you've enjoyed discussing accounting for options grants. So I'm curious what's your view of the new accounting standard which mandates that companies report lower tax provisions based on so-called excess tax benefits enjoyed when shared-based compensation ends up being more profitable for the grantees than what is initially modeled. These so-called excess benefits used to go to the shareholders equity line on the balance sheet. Which accounting method makes more sense to you – the old method or the new?

Warren: Johnny, I think you know more about that than I do. So if I were asked to answer that question I'd probably call you up and say what should I say. It's not a factor that will enter into Berkshire. So I really have not, ... I mean, I've heard just a little bit about the accounting standard but I really don't know anything about it.

Charlie?

Charlie: It's not a big deal, Warren.

Warren: Oh yeah, I know that. [laughter]. There are a few things in accounting we really disagree with and whether they might be material, for example, to somebody trying to evaluate Berkshire. That primarily gets into amortization of intangibles. It certainly gets them to realize capital gains and that sort of thing. And we will go to great lengths to try to tell our partners basically - not all of whom are accounting experts or anything. We will try to make clear to them, at least, what our view is - the same way as if I had a family business and I was talking to my sisters or something about it.

Unless it is material, we'll probably stay away from trying to opine on any new accounting standards. If it's material to Berkshire, we will go to great lengths to, at least, give our view.
Charlie?

Charlie: I certainly agree with that.

Warren: OK....

Charlie: What he's talking about is not very material to Berkshire.

Warren: No, it isn't and it really won't be.

Charlie: No.

Warren: Some of these others are though. We will bring those up as they come up. We are reporting $400 and some million less in our earnings than if Precision Castparts had remained a public company. Well, with Precision Castparts, I mean, are the earnings less real? Is the cash less real? Is anything less because it's moved the ownership? I don't think so. And I want to convey that belief to shareholders and they can debate whether it's right or wrong.

I think it's a mistake not to comment and just assume that the owners understand that; because it is a fairly arcane point so we pointed it out. But we also pointed out if we think depreciation is inadequate for valuation purposes - that depreciation is as inadequate at a very capital intensive business like BNSF which we, I must say, still love anyway.

Charlie, anymore?

Charlie: No.

Warren: Okay, Section 5.

MARKET VALUATION

Q48. Audience, Station 5: Thank you and good afternoon. I'm Adam Burgman with Sterling Capital in Virginia Beach, Virginia. Earlier today Mr. Munger commented on the valuation of China versus the U.S. market. My question for you is are market cap to GDP and cyclically adjusted P/E still valid ways to consider market valuation and how do those influence Berkshire's investment decisions? Thank you.

Warren: I would say that both of the standards you mentioned are not paramount at all in our valuation of securities. It's harder. People are always looking for a formula and there is an ultimate formula. But the trouble is you don't know what to stick into the variables. But the value of anything is the present value of all the cash it is ever going to distribute. But the P/E ratios, ..., every number has some degree of meaning - means more sometimes than another.

Valuation of a business is not reducible to any formula where you can actually put in the variables perfectly. And both of the things that you mentioned themselves get bandied around a lot. It's not that they're unimportant. But sometimes they are going to be very important, sometimes it can be almost totally unimportant. It's just not quite as simple as as having one or two formulas and then saying the market is undervalued or overvalued or a company is undervalued or overvalued.

The most important thing is future interest rates. And people frequently plug in the current interest rate saying that's the best they can do; after all it does reflect the market's judgment. And, you know, the 30-year bond should tell you what people who are willing to put up money for 30 years and have no risk of dollar gain or dollar loss at the end of the 30 year period. But what better figure can you come up with. I'm not sure and come up with a better figure but that doesn't mean I want to use the current figure either. So I would say that I think Charlie's anawer will be that he does not come up with China versus the US market based on what you've mentioned as yardsticks. But now Charlie you tell him.

Charlie: All I meant was, as I said before, that the first rule of fishing is to fish where the fish are. It's that a good fisherman can find more fish in China, if fishes is the stock market. That's all I meant. It's a happier hunting ground.

Warren: This doesn't relate directly but I just want to go back to one question tht was mentioned earlier. I really think, if you want to be a good evaluator of businesses and investor, you really ought to figure out a way, without too much personal damage, to run a lousy business for a while. I think you'll learn a whole lot more about business by actually struggling with a terrible business for a couple of years than you learn by getting into a very good one where the business itself is so good they can't mess it up. I don't know whether Charlie has a view on it or not but it certainly was a big part of our learning experience. And I think a bigger part, in the sense that being involved with good business was actually being involved in some bad businesses, and just seeing...

Charlie: How awful it was.

Warren: ... how awful it is and how little you can do about it. And that our I.Q. does not solve the problem in a whole bunch of things. It's a useful experience but I wouldn't advise too much of it. So, what do you think, Charlie here?

Charlie: It was very useful to us. There's nothing like personal painful experience, if you want to learn. And we certainly had our share of it.

Warren: OK, Becky?

MAJOR RISK FOR BERKSHIRE

Q49. Journalist, Becky Quick: This question comes from Tom Spenvilere and he'd like to be called Tom Spenn from Pennsylvania. He says in life, business, and investing strategies often work until they don't work. Other than a massive insurance loss, any thoughts on what could cause the Berkshire enterprise to not work.

Warren: I think the only ...

Charlie: Good question.

Warren: Well, if there were some change, if we got some infection - outside agent of some sort to change the culture in some major way, an invasion of different thought. But as a practical matter, I don't think anything – you know, it's the things you can't think of - but I can't think of anything that can harm Berkshire in a material permanent way except weapons of mass destruction. But I don't regard that as a low probability. It would take a recession, a depression, a panic, hurricanes, earthquakes. They all would have some effect and in some cases it might even be that we would do better because of them. But if there were a successful, as measured by the aggressor, nuclear, chemical, biological or cyber attack on the United States (and there are plenty of people who would like to pull that off - or organizations and maybe even a few countries). It could disrupt society to such an extent that it would harm us. But I think with the variety of earnings streams, with the asset positions, with the general philosophy in place, I think we would be very close to the last one affected. But if somebody figures out how to kill millions of Americans and totally disrupt society then all bets are off.

Charlie?

Charlie: Well I agree it would take something really extreme. And just take the question like British Petroleum took a huge loss with one oil well blowing. And Berkshire has all these independent subsidiaries and they really are independent. The parent company is not alarmed if there's one horrible accident somewhere. We would tend to pay, of course; maybe more than our legal liability. But we are not one accident and one subsidiary that caused a lot of damage. We are better protected than most companies.

Warren: Yeah.

Charlie: In every way, Berkshire is structured to handle stresses.

Warren: It's the kind of thing we think about all the time we've thought about it ever since we started. But I really don't know any company that could take more general adversity or even some specific adversities. But if you get into what could happen with weapons of mass destruction, that is something we can't protect against. But if that ever happens, there'll be more to worry than the price of Berkshire.

Jay?

PROPERTY AND CASUALTY INSURANCE

Q50. Analyst, Jay: Berkshire Hathaway Specialty Insurance generated $1.3 billion of premium volume in 2016. This business is on the smaller end of commercial property casualty insurers in terms of scale although its volume did grow 40 percent last year. In a highly competitive commercial P&C environment, what gives you confidence that Berkshire Hathaway Specialty is destined to become one of the world's leading commercial P&C insurers, as you said in this year's annual letter?

Warren: I think it will be and I think how fast it grows depends very much on the market. I mean we are not interested in trying to be a price cutter in a market where the prices already aren't that attractive. But we have built the scale worldwide in a lot of this has been added in recent months, just over the past year.

We will grow a lot. If the market should turn hard for any reason we would grow a lot faster. But we are destined at Berkshire Hathaway Specialty to be one of the leading P&C firms in the world, just as we were destined to have - when Ajit came in even though we had nothing - we were destined to become a very important reinsurer throughout the world and, in certain ways, almost the only reinsurer for certain types of risk in the world.

We've got the people, we've got the capital, we've got the reputation. There is no stronger company in the insurance world and there won't be than that Berkshire Hathaway insurers. We've got the talent there. So it will grow. It may grow slowly some years it may show big jumps just like the reinsurance operation did many years ago. But it's a very important position to Berkshire that brought that on. We just wish we could have started a little earlier but you have to have the right people and they came to us and, as you said, we wrote - whatever it was - a billion three ($1.3 billion) or a billion four ($1.4 billion) last year and we'll write more this year. But we won't write as much as if we were in a hard market.

Station 6.

"... medical costs are the tapeworm of American economic competitiveness... it is not the tax system that is crippling Berkshire's competitiveness around the world or anything of this sort. Our health costs have gone up incredibly and will go up a lot more."
Warren Buffett

"I really like teaching. Basically, I've been doing it formally and you can say, somewhat informally, all my life and I certainly had the greatest teachers you can imagine. So, if somebody thought that I did a decent job of teaching I'd feel very good about that."
Warren Buffett

"Bismarck said there are two things that nobody should have to watch. One was the making of sausage and the other is the making of legislation."
Charlie Munger

LEARNING MACHINE

Q51. Audience, Station 6: Good afternoon. My name is Sally Burns. I'm from Australia but I currently reside in Austin, Texas. My question, Mr. Buffett, I have heard that Mr. Munger says your greatest talent is actually a learning machine. That you never stop updating your views. What are the most interesting things you've learned over the last few years?

Warren: Well, it is fun to learn. Charlie is much more of a learning machine than I am. I'm a specialized one. He does as much as I do in my specialty and then he's got a much more general absorption rate than I have about what's going on in the world. But, you know, it's a world that gets more fascinating all the time. And a lot of fun can occur when you learn you were wrong on something. That's when you really learn that your old ideas really weren't so correct and you have to adapt to new ones and that, of course, is difficult.

I think, actually, what's going on in America is terribly terribly interesting and politically all kinds of things. Just the way the world is unfolding. It's moving fast. I do enjoy trying to figure out not only what's going to happen but what's even happening now. But I don't think I've got any special insights that would be useful to you. But maybe Charlie does.

Charlie: Well, I think buying the Apple stock is a good sign in Warren. And now he did run around Omaha as he was, he would take his grandchildren's tablets away. He did market research and I do think we keep learning and, more important, we keep (we don't unlearn) the old tricks and that is really important.

You look at the people who try and solve their problems by printing money and lying and so forth. Take Puerto Rico; who would have guessed a territory in the United States would be in bankruptcy. Oh, I would have predicted it; because they behaved like idiots. [laughter].

Warren: So, we did not buy any Puerto Rico bonds.

Charlie: No. And you go to Europe and look at the government bond portfolios we are required to hold in Europe. There are no Greek bonds and the bonds of nobody but Germany. Just everywhere you look in Berkshire somebody is being sensible and that is a great pleasure. Combine that with being very opportunistic so that when something comes along - like a panic - it's a nice. It's like playing with two hands instead of one in a game that requires two hands. It helps to have a fair-sized repertoire and, Warren, we've learned so damn much. There are all kinds of things we've done in the last 10 years we would not have gotten 20 years ago.

Warren: Yeah, that's true although ... - I've mentioned this before - one of the best books on investment was written, I think, in 1958. I think I read it in around 1960 by Phil Fisher called *Common Stocks and Uncommon Profits* and...

Charlie: In all those companies went dead eventually.

Warren: But it talked about the importance or the usefulness of what he called the "scuttlebutt method." And you know that was something I didn't learn from Graham but every now and then it's turned out to be very useful. It doesn't solve everything and I mean there's a whole lot more he says.

Charlie: Oh I saw that you did it with American Express in the salad oil scandal just as you did it with Apple decades later.

Warren: In certain cases you actually can learn a lot just by asking a lot of questions and I give Philip Fisher credit. That book goes back a lot of years. But, as Charlie said some of the companies he picked as winners forever, that did sort of peter out on him. But the basic idea is - that you can learn a lot of things just by asking, in some cases. I mean if I got interested in the coal industry, just say to pick one out of the air, and when I was much younger and more energetic, if I went and talked to the heads of ten coal companies and I asked each one of them - way later into the conversation after they really felt like talking - I would just say "if you had to go away for 10 years on a desert island and you had to put all of your family's money into one of your competitors which one would it be and why?" And then I'd ask them if they had to sell short one of their competitors for 10 years, based on all their family money and why. Everybody loves talking about their competitors and if you do that with ten different companies, you'll probably have a better fix on the economics of the coal industry than any one of those individuals has.

There are ways of getting at things and sometimes they're useful, sometimes they're not. But sometimes they can be very useful. And the idea of just learning more all the time about ... I am more specialized by far than Charlie. He wants to learn about everything and I just want to learn about something that will help Berkshire. It's a very useful attitude to have toward the world and, of course, I don't know who said it but somebody said "the problem is not in getting the new ideas but in shedding the old ones" and there's a lot of truth to that.

Charlie: We would never have Iscar if it had come along 10 years earlier. We would never have bought Precision Castparts if it had come along 10 years earlier. We are learning and, my God, we're still learning.

Warren: OK, Andrew.

HEALTH CARE PROBLEMS

Q52. Journalist, Andrew Ross Sorkin: Hi Warren, this is my final question. In 2012 you were quoted as saying "I think the health care problem is the number one problem of America and of American business." We have not dealt with that yet. Do you believe that the current administration's plan to repeal and replace ACA will ultimately benefit the economy and Berkshire or not?

Warren: Well, I'll answer. I'll give you two answers here. The first one being that if you go back to 1960 or thereabouts corporate taxes were about 4 percent of GDP. They bounced around some and now they're about 2 percent of GDP and at that time health care was 5 percent of GDP and now it's about 17 percent of GDP. So when American business talks about taxes strangling our competitiveness and that sort of thing, they're talking about something that as a percentage of GDP has gone down from four to two while medical costs, which are borne to a great extent by business, have gone from 5 to 17 percent. So medical costs are the tapeworm of American economic competitiveness.

If you're really talking about it - and that business knows that they don't feel they can do much about it. But it is not the tax system is crippling Berkshire's competitiveness around the world or anything of the sort. Our health costs have

gone up incredibly and will go up a lot more. And if you look at the rest of the world, there were half a dozen countries that were around our 5 percent, if you go back to the earlier years, and while we are 17 now, they are 10 or 11 percent. So, they have gained a five or six point advantage in the world, even in those countries with fairly high medical costs.
Charlie: and with socialized medicine.

Warren: Yeah. So it's a huge ...

Whatever I said then goes and is accentuated now. That is the problem that society is having trouble with it and is going to have more trouble with. Regardless of which party is in power, anything of the sort, it almost transcends that.

In terms of the new Act that was passed a couple of days ago versus the Obama Administration Act, it's a very interesting thing. All I can tell you is the net effect of that Act on one person is that my federal income taxes would have gone down 17 percent last year if what was proposed went into effect. So, it is a huge tax cut for guys like me and you have to figure out the effects of the rest of the Act but the one thing I can tell you is if it goes through the way the House put it, anybody with $250,000 dollars a year of adjusted gross income and a lot of investment income is going to have a huge tax cut. And when there's a tax cut either the deficit goes up or they get the taxes from somebody else. As it stands now, that is the one predictable effect if it should pass and the Senate will do something different or go to conference, and who knows what happens. But that is in the law that was passed a couple of days ago.

Charlie?

Charlie: Well I certainly agree with you about the medical care. What I don't like about the medical care is we are getting too much medicine. There is too much chemotherapy on people that are all but dead and all kinds of crazy things going on in Medicare and other parts of the health system. And there are so many vested interests that it's very hard to change. But I don't think any rational person looking objectively from the outside of the American system of medical care ...

We all love the new lifesaving stuff and the new chemotherapies and the new drugs and all that. But, my God, this system is crazy and the cost is just going wild. And it does put our manufacturers at a big disadvantage with other people where the government is paying the medical costs, and And so I agree with Warren totally.

Warren: If you had to bet 10 years for it if it will be higher or lower than 17 percent of GDP?

Charlie: Well, if present trends continue it will get more and more. There are huge vested interests in having this thing continue the way it is. And they're very vocal and active and the rest of us are indifferent. So naturally we get a terrible result. And I would say that on this issue both parties hate each other so much that neither one of them can think rationally. And I don't think that helps either. [applause].

Warren: It is kind of interesting that the federal government spends or raises I will say, three and a half trillion or something like that. I mean the degree of concern everybody has about that although that's stayed fairly steady in the 18 percent or so of GDP plus or minus a couple points. But three trillion plus is spent on health care and everybody

160

wants the best and it's perfectly understandable. But it's a very very big number compared to the whole federal budget.

There's some overlap and all of that but if you talk about world competitiveness of American industry, it's the biggest single variable where we keep getting more and more out of whack with the rest of the world and it's very very tough for political parties to attack it. Basically it's a political subject of a lot of...

Charlie: It is deeply immoral. If you have a group of hospital people and doctors that are feasting like a bunch of jackals on the carcass of some dying person, it's not a pretty sight. [applause].

Warren: Tell them about that group in California ...

Charlie: Oh yeah. That is Redding [California]. This is one of my favorite stories. There are a bunch of very ambitious cardiologists and heart surgeons in Redding and they got the thought that really a heart was a widowmaker. So everybody, every patient, that came in they said "you've got a widow maker in your chest and we know how to fix it." And so they recommended heart surgery for everybody. And, of course, they developed a huge volume of heart surgery and they got very wonderful results because nobody comes through heart surgery better than the man who doesn't need it at all. [laughter]. And they made so much money that the hospital chain which was tenant brought all its other hospitals. "Why can't you be more like Redding?" And - it's a true story - it went on and on and on and finally there was some fellow, a beloved Catholic priest, and they said "you've got a widowmaker in your chest" and he didn't believe them and he blew the whistle.

Warren: He is a priest. You can see why he didn't believe them. [laughter].

Charlie: At any rate, when you get a routine you just keep using it. If the heart is a widowmaker it's a widowmaker.

Later, I met one of the doctors who threw these people out of the medical profession and I said to him "in the end, did they think they were doing anything wrong?" He said "No, Charlie. They thought that what they were doing was good for people." That is why it is so hard to fix these things. The self ... the delusion that comes into people as they make money and get more successful by doing all kinds of awful things, should never be underestimated. [applause].

A lot of that goes on and you come under such gross craziness and you would have thought little Wells Fargo looks like innocencts when they have their little trouble with their incentive system. But the heart surgery rate was 20 times normal or something! You'd think you'd notice if you're running a hospital. But they did not notice it but wanted the other hospitals to be more like it.

Warren: They had a terrific success ratio.

OK, Gregg.

BERKSHIRE HATHAWAY ENERGY

Q53. Analyst, Gregg Warren: Thank you. Warren. As you look forward, and taking into consideration some of the headwinds facing the U.S. based utilities, including:

- **weaker electricity demand growth as increasing energy efficiency impacts demand;**

- distributed generation which hits vertically integrated utilities doubly hard as they face both declining energy sales revenue and increased network costs to support reliable delivery; and
- third, higher interest rates which would increase borrowing costs,

what are the key attributes that Berkshire Energy would be looking for in future acquisition candidates?

In particular, are there advantages or disadvantage attached to, say, transmission assets relative to generation assets that would make you favor one over the other?

Warren: Yeah, well generation assets, you can say, are inherently have more risk because some of them are going to …

Charlie: be stranded

Warren: … be stranded or obsolete. The question is how they are going to treat the stranded and all that sort of thing. We, on the other hand, have more of the capital in the generating assets so that tends to be where a good bit of the capital base is. We like the utility business OK. I mean the electricity demand is not increasing like it was as you point out. There are going to be stranded assets. If they are stranded because of rank foolishness, the utility commission will be less inclined to let you figure that in your rate base as you go forward, as opposed to things that are more societal.

Demands are just changing but we still think the utility business is a very decent asset. The prices are very high. But that's what happens in a low interest rate environment. I would be surprised if 10 years from now, we don't have significantly more money in not only wind and solar but we probably own more utility systems than we own now.

We are a buyer of choice with many utility commissions. In fact, we can put up the slide. There's a slide which shows something about our pricing compared to other utilities. Greg Abel and his group have done an extraordinary job. They've done it in safety, they've done it in reliability, they've done it in price and they've done it in renewables. It's hard to imagine a better run operation than exists at Mid-American Energy and people want us with that record. People want us to come to their state in many many cases. But when prices get to the level they have - some utilities are sold at extraordinary prices and we can't pay them and have it make sense to Berkshire shareholders. But just because we can't do it this year doesn't mean it won't happen next year or the year after. So I think we'll get a chance.

Charlie: And our utilities are not normal. The way Greg has run those things, they're so much better run in every way than normal utilities. They're better regarded by the paying customers, they are better regarded by the regulators, they have better safety records. Everything about it is way the hell better and it's a pleasure to be associated with people like that and to have assets of that quality. And it's a lot safer. If somebody asked Berkshire to build a $50 billion dollar nuclear plant we wouldn't do it.

Warren: We have public power here in Nebraska and it's been sort of the pride of Nebraska for many decades. There are no privately-held utility systems and it's totally public power. Those utilities have no requirements for earnings on equity. They can borrow at tax exempt rates, we have to borrow taxable rates and Nebraska is not that much different than that Iowa and we're selling electricity across the river a few miles from here at lower prices than exist in Nebraska. So, it's an extraordinary utility and it was lucky when we got involved in it then. I thank Walter Scott, our director, for introducing me to it almost 17 or 18 years ago or so. But I don't think the utility business as such - I mean if I were putting together a portfolio of stocks - I don't think there would be any utilities in that group now. But I love the fact that we own Berkshire Hathaway Energy.

Charlie: But it's different, radically different and better.

Warren: A lot better, actually.

Station 7.

MCLANE COMPANY INC.

Q54. Audience, Station 7: My name is Gren Misterly from beautiful historic St. Augustine, Florida. I've been a fan of yours and Berkshire since I was a kid looking through the stock pages and seeing one crazy stock that traded for ten thousand dollars a share. Unfortunately, I wasn't able to convince my parents to buy it at that point. But now I'm a shareholder as an adult. I'm here with my daughters Mabel who is 7, Willow who's 1 year old, and my wife. I graciously read the letter every year and I love the stories from the different companies: GEICO and See's, BNSF, that kind of teach investing lessons. And this year when I was looking through the accounting information in the back I noticed that one company McLane contributes a lot of revenue, a large portion of Berkshire's revenue and, to a lesser extent, earnings. But I don't ever see much about it in the annual report. So I'm curious why we don't hear more about that company and are there any investing lessons

like we get from See's and GEICO that you can share about that company?

Warren: Yeah, McLane. The reason you see their figures separately is because the FCC has certain requirements that are based on sales and McLane is a company that has an extraordinary amount of sales in relation to intrinsic value or to net income. It basically is a distributor of ... well, it's a huge customer, for example, for the food companies, the candy companies, the cigarette companies that go up and down the line of anything that goes into convenience stores.

We bought it from Wal-Mart and Wal-Mart is our biggest customer. I can't tell you the precise volume but if you put Wal-Mart and Sams together, you're getting up to 20 percent plus. It's nationwide but in the end it operates on about 6 percent gross margins and 5 percent operating expenses. So it has a 1 percent pre-tax margin and obviously a 1 percent pre-tax margin only works in terms of return on capital if you turn your equity extraordinarily fast. And that's what McLane does. Being a wholesaler, it's moving things in and moving things out, very fast, very efficiently. It also has a few liquor distribution subsidiaries that have wider margins but the basic McLane business is $45 billion plus and makes 1 percent pre-tax on sales but the return on capital is very decent. It sort of has an outsized appearance simply because of this huge volume of sales that go through.

Grady Rosier who runs it is exceptional. He was there when we bought it from Wal-Mart whatever it was a dozen years ago. And I've been there once. We've got thousands and thousands of trucks, big distribution centers all over the country. It is a major factor in moving goods at wholesale. I mean if you're in Mars candy or something of the sort, I mean we will be the biggest customer but that pretty well describes the business.

It's a business that earns good returns in relation to invested capital and in relation to our purchase price. But every tenth of a cent is important in the business. Moving your receivables exceptionally fast and consequently you have payables moving big time. So, the sales are 30 times receivables and 30 times payables. You've got maybe 35 or so times inventory. I mean this is a business that is moving a lot of goods. It's an important subsidiary but not as remotely as important as would be indicated by the by the sales; still, very important in terms of making the kind of money that shows up in the 10-K.

Charlie?

Charlie: You said it all.

Warren: That was an interesting thing: Wal-Mart wanted to sell it. They came to see us and we made a deal and the CFO came. We talked for a while. He went into the other room, called the CEO and came back and said "you have a deal." And Wal-Mart has told me subsequently that they never had a deal that close as fast as the one with Berkshire. We said what we would pay. It was cash. And we got it done very promptly and they were terrific on their side.

Charlie: By the way, that reputation for being quick and simple and doing what we promised and so on has helped Berkshire time after time.

Warren: Yeah yeah, we wouldn't have made that deal without essentially having that reputation. But they knew …

Charlie: We bought the Northern Natural Gas Company in one weekend and they wanted the money on Monday.

Warren: They needed the money on Monday.

Charlie: Before the lawyers could complete the legal papers. We managed to do it.

Warren: Well, not only that but I think it took some clearance in Washington and, essentially, I think I wrote a letter and said that if they decided after looking at it they didn't want to clear it, we're already done doing the deal and these guys needed the money so badly we were going to give them the money. So, essentially, based on the deal clearing and there wasn't any reason why it wouldn't clear but there was just a procedural problem.

Most companies can't do that. But we can. We've got the flexibility that really in most large companies just plain doesn't exist; or too many people have to sign off on something of that sort. So the Northern Natural deal would not have been made if we had to follow the normal timetable.

Charlie: And it's a lovely business to own.

Warren: Yeah, absolutely.

Now we are moving from one station to another between now and 3:30. So we now go to Station 8.

LEGACY OF CHARLIE MUNGER

Q55. Audience, Station 8: Good morning or good afternoon, Warren and Charlie.

Warren: Hi.

Audience: Jai Norwood from West Des Moines, Iowa. You guys have iron bladders. [laughter].

Warren: We won't tell you the secret to that. [laughter].

Audience: Wondering about a contraption under the table.

Warren: No, no, you can come down and inspect.

Audience: I have a question for each. Warren, I was fortunate to ask you a question I think in 2011 about legacy - what you wanted to be known for 100 years from now and I'm kind of curious to hear what Charlie would like to be known for. Warren I'm 52 so I guess you started doing this when I was born. And I'm kind of interested in a memory from your first annual meeting.

Charlie: My first memory when Warren got on the subject and they asked him what would he want said at his funeral. He said "I want them to all be saying that's the oldest looking corpse I ever saw." [laughter].

Warren: That maybe the smartest thing I ever said. With me, it's very simple. I really like teaching. Basically, I've been doing it formally and you can say, somewhat informally, all my life and I certainly had the greatest teachers you can imagine. So, if somebody thought that I did a decent job of teaching I'd feel very good about that. [applause].

Charlie: Yeah. And to make the teaching endurable, you have to have a bit of wise-assery in it and that we've both been able to supply.

Warren: And for those of you who are old time basketball fans, I might mention that on Wilt Chamberlain's tomb, it reputed it was going to say, "at last I sleep alone." [laughter]. Ok, Station 9.

BUFFETT'S AND MUNGER'S DREAM

Q56. Audience, Station 9: Good afternoon Mr. Munger and Mr. Buffett. My name is a Xioyai. I come from China. It's my first time to come to this meeting and I think I'm very lucky to have a chance to ask a question.

Warren: We're glad to have you.

Audience: Thank you. Everyone has personal dreams and at different ages the dreams may be different. What's your dream now?

Warren: Charlie?

Charlie: I didn't quite hear that.

Warren: What's your dream now?

Charlie: My dream. [laughter].

Warren: Let's skip the first one. [laughter].

Charlie: Sometimes when I'm especially wishful I think "oh to be 90 again." [laughter]. And I've got some advice for the young. If you've got anything you really want to do, don't wait till you're 93.

Warren: Do it. That's the same thing I would tell students. You can't always find it the first time or the second time but when you go out in the world, look for the job that you would take if you didn't need a job. Don't postpone, that sort of thing. Somebody, I think Kierkegaard, said that life must be evaluated backwards but it must be lived forwards and you want to sort of - Charlie says all he wants to know is where he will die, so he will never go there [laughter] - you do want to do a certain amount of reverse engineering in life. That tdoesn't you can do everything that way but you really want to think about what will make you feel good, when you get older, about your life. And, generally, you want to keep going in that direction. You need some luck in life and you've got to accept some bad things that are going to happen as you go along. But life has been awfully good to me and Charlie. So we have no complaints.

Charlie: What you don't want to be is like the man who when they held this funeral and Minister said, "now is the time for somebody to say something nice about the deceased" and nobody came forward, ... and nobody came forward. Then he said, "surely somebody can say something nice about the deceased." Stilll, nobody came forward. And finally one man came up and he said "well ...", he said "his brother was worse." [laughter].

Warren: OK, we'll move to station 10 and see if we can improve on that.

EBITDA – EARNINGS BEFORE INTEREST, TAXES, DEPRECIATION AND AMORTIZATION

Q57. Audience, Station 10: Hi, My name is Andy from Innovation Capital from Shanghai. This is my sixth year from Shanghai to here. I have to say to you two, Warren and Charlie, you are highly respected and deeply loved by millions and millions or even billions globally. I have

171

two questions today. First question, in your letters to shareholders, you said you believe **EBITDA** is not a good parameter to value a business. Why is that? Can you elaborate on that? Second question. You both have very successful and happy lives. With great respect, my question is to each of you: in retrospect from a personal standpoint, do you have regrets in life? If there is one thing you would have done differently in your life – family, personal or business - what is it? Thank you very much.

Warren: Yeah. I don't think you should expect us to answer that on personal. But in business, I would say I wish I had met Charlie earlier. We've had a lot of fun ever since I was 29 and he was 35. But it would have been even more fun if we had started that many many years earlier. We had a chance to; we worked in the same grocery store but not at the same time.

With respect to EBITDA, depreciation is an expense. It's the worst kind of expense. You know we love to talk about float and float is where we get the money first and we have the expense later. Depreciation is where you spend the money first and then record the expense later and it's reverse float and it's not a good thing; and to have that entered into a multiple ... [for example, Price to EBITDA].

It is much better to buy a business that has - everything else being equal - has no depreciation because it has essentially no investment in fixed assets and makes X than it is to buy a company where there's a lot of depreciation and getting X.

Acctually I may write a little bit more on that next year just because it's such a mass delusion and, of course, it's in the interest of Wall Street, enormously, to focus on something called the EBITDA because it results in higher borrowing power, higher valuations and all of that sort of thing. So it's become very popular in the last 20 years. But it's a very misleading statistic and can be used in very pernicious ways.

Chartlie, what do you think on one of those subjects?

Charlie: I think you've understated the horrors of the subject and the disgusting nature of the people that brought that term into the valuation of business. It would be like a leasing broker of real estate who has a 1,000 square foot suite to be leased and he says it's got 2,000 square feet in it. That's not honorable behavior and that's the way that term got into common usage. Nobody in his right mind would think that depreciation is not an expense.

Warren: But it's very much in the interests of Wall Street.

Charlie: Yes that's why they did it.

Warren: Yeah.

Charlie: It made the multiple seem lower.

Warren: And what's amazing is the way it's accepted actually. But anyway, it just illustrates how people use language and sell concepts that work to their own use. 2-and-20 [common hedge fund fee structure] has the same sort of thing. I mean the number of people … the amount of money that over perform after paying 2-and-20 compared to the expenses that have been incurred, I will show you, makes for a terrible indictment of that particular arrangement. But as long as it can get sold it will get sold.

Charlie: And now they use it in the business schools. That is horror squared. I mean, it's bad enough that a bunch of thieves are using a term but when it gets so common that business schools copy it – that is not a good result.

OK, [applause] Station 11.

RELOCATION OF BUSINESSES OVERSEAS

Q58. Audience, Station 11: Good afternoon. I'm Whitney Tilson a shareholder from New York. My question is related to the ones I asked earlier about job cuts. Perhaps the only thing that makes American workers angrier than lay offs is to shut down an operation entirely and move the jobs overseas. Ask anyone in Ohio or Michigan and they'll tell you stories about companies that have been operating in those states for decades benefiting from the educational system, infrastructure and so forth. Things that were paid for by local taxpayers but then some high paid consultants came along and showed the company how it could reduce its costs by relocating production to Mexico or China and poof the good U.S. jobs disappear. My observation is that most investors and those in corporate America today worship at the altar of maximizing shareholder value which is code for doing whatever is necessary to boost the share price as high as possible. But in doing so companies are taking actions that make millions of workers feel, at best, fearful and left behind and, at worst, deeply harmed by corporate America. It makes so many people so angry that I think it's testing the post World War II economic order which is rooted in free trade and even the strength of our democracy. I'd argue that it was decisive in our last election. So my question to you is do you think that businesses should consider factors outside of pure economics when making these types of decisions? What obligations, if any, do they have to their employees and communities in which they operate? And, lastly, if a Berkshire CEO came to you and asked for your approval to close the U.S. operation and relocate it overseas to save money, what questions would you ask beyond the economics of this decision? Thank you.

Warren: Yeah, well, the truth is that in certain cases production that otherwise would formerly have been in the United States has definitely been supplanted by production that comes from other parts of the world. Originally, I was there when Fruit of the Loom, once called Union Underwear was bought by Graham Newman Corp. in 1955, I believe and it was probably all domestic then. And the truth is if it was all domestic now it wouldn't exist. We had the same thing happen with Dexter Shoe another wonderful company, and skilled workers and in the end we sold the shoes at a price that yielded what they cost us. They were not competitive with shoes from around the world.

Trade, I would argue both ways, export import, massive trade should be and is actually enormously beneficial both to the United States and to the world. Greater productivity will benefit the world in a general way. But to be roadkill, to be the textile worker in New Bedford that was put out of a job eventually, to be shoe worker in Dexter to be put out of work is, I mean, it would be no fun to go through life and say "hey I'm doing this for the greater good so that shoes or underwear would sell for 5 percent less or something" and the American public will actually never know. So what you need is two things in my view. You've got an enormously prosperous country, you've got almost $60,000 of GDP per capita. It's unbelievable, six times what it was when I was born, in real terms. So we've got the prosperity and that prosperity is enhanced by trade. We were only exporting 5 percent of our GDP back in 1970 and now, I think, it's around 12 percent or something like that.

We are doing what we do best but we need an Educator-in-Chief who logically is the President (and I don't mean this specific President). I mean, any president that has been around for decades has to be able to explain to the American public the overall benefits of, essentially, free trade and then beyond that we have to have policies that take care of the people that become the roadkill in the process; because it doesn't make any difference to me, as far as I'm concerned, if my life is miserable because I've been put out of business by something that's good for 320 million people in some infinitesimal way and it's messed up my life when I've tried to live it in a proper way. So we have got the resources to take care of those people. The investors I don't worry about.

I wrote about this few years ago. Investors can diversify their investments in such a way that, overall, trade probably benefits them and they don't get killed by a specific industry condition. But the worker, in many cases, can't do that. You are not going to retrain some 55 year old worker in New Bedford who may not even speak English in our textile mill or something. If they get destroyed by something that's good for society they get destroyed unless government puts in some policies that take care of people like that and we've got to do that and we've got a rich society that can do that and we've got a society that will benefit by free trade and I think we ought to try to hit both objectives of making sure that there is not road kill and that at the same time we get 320 million people get the benefits of free trade. [applause].

Charlie?

Charlie: Well, I don't quarrel with that. We have unemployment insurance for that exact reason. But, I'm afraid, that a capitalist system is always going to hurt some people as it modifies and improves. There's no way to avoid it.

Warren: Well, capitalism is brutal to capital if you are in the wrong businesses and, like I say, you can diversify those results. Capitalism is brutal to the people that have the bad luck to be skilled or develop their skills for decades but a very rich society can actually - if it's beneficial to society overall - it can take care of those people. The new tax bill that was passed a couple of days ago reduces my taxes by 17 percent, you know. Is that needed by the government?

Charlie: I wouldn't start spending the money.

Warren: No. But that was, ... I mean no, I agree. I don't know, ... who knows what happens with the bill but I'm just ... to have that happen and I don't think that. I think if you polled 1,000 people in Omaha that were walking through a shopping center as to whether my tax bill or some very large sum because of what passed I don't think many people would have the faintest idea what happened there in terms of the coverage of it and all that that took place. We do have probably more like $57,000 or $68,000 of GDP per capita, a family of four: $230,000. But nobody should be roadkill in this.

Charlie: Bismarck said there are two things that nobody should have to watch. One was the making of sausage and the other is the making of legislation.

Warren: Well, I would say that somebody ought to watch.

Anyway, we get the magic hour 3:30. We'll reconvene at 3:45 to have a formal shareholders meeting and that may take a while. So you're welcome to stay and watch that or you're welcome to shop and I might even have a small preference for that that but go and do whatever you wish, OK.

End of Q&A session

"Nothing to add"
Charlie Munger

Epilogue

If you regularly read the writings of Warren Buffett and Charlie Munger and pay attention to their teachings on life and business, there is no question that the only outcome will be to grow in wisdom. Their combination of high ethical standards and astute business acumen is rare. As aptly stated by Bill Gates, a member of the Berkshire Hathaway board, the weekend of the AGM "is one of the most enjoyable 'duties' of my year." [3] We agree. Attending Berkshire Hathaway shareholders' meeting is one of the best ways to spend a weekend. We consider Warren Buffett's letters to the shareholders and their (Warren's and Charlie's) answers to the questions at the AGM as the best lessons in finance and investment.

You are probably reading this book because you see yourself as a student of value investing, specifically registered in the school of Warren Buffett and Charlie Munger. We hope if you attended the 2017 shareholder meeting, this book has been a refresher and you now have a record of it so that you can revisit Warren's and Charlie's perspectives on the questions that were asked. If you were not able to attend the meeting, then this is your access to the Q&A session. We hope this format will continue and we will continue to learn from these legends.

We expect the 2018 meeting to be equally informative, enlightening, fascinating, and fun. As always, we expect investment wisdom that is certainly worth keeping record of. Warren and Charlie always have unusual but accurate perspectives of business and finance and it will be worth your while to hear them in their own words. We will

---

[3] http://www.gatesnotes.com/About-Bill-Gates/Master-Class-with-Warren-Buffett-Berkshire-Hathaway-Annual-Meeting-2014

continue to do our best to take accurate notes and to present them in a reader-friendly form.

About the Authors

Eben Otuteye

Eben Otuteye is Professor of Finance at the University of New Brunswick, Fredericton, Canada. Professor Otuteye joined the Faculty of Business Administration at UNB in 1987 where he has been teaching various finance courses, including principles of finance, corporate finance, investments, value investing, personal financial planning, and theory of finance, in both the BBA and MBA programs.

Dr. Otuteye's research interests include behavioral finance, value investing, asset pricing models, portfolio management strategies, and the economics of e-business, topics on which he has made many conference presentations all over the world and published in several high-ranking journals.

In collaboration with Mohammad Siddiquee, Professor Otuteye developed a heuristic (the O-S heuristic) for making value investing decisions. This is a system that incorporates the value investing principles as originally propounded by Benjamin Graham and its extensions as developed and practiced by Warren Buffett and Charlie Munger.

Mohammad Siddiquee

Mohammad Siddiquee is an Assistant Professor of Finance at the Department of Business Administration, Tourism and Hospitality Management at the Mount Saint Vincent University. His research focuses on behavioural finance as well as the psychology of decision-making, particularly in investment management.

Influenced by the works of Benjamin Graham and his disciple Warren Buffett, Dr. Siddiquee also studies value investing and has co-developed a simple value investing decision-making tool. He received his MBA in 2012 and PhD in 2017 from the University of New Brunswick.

Dr. Siddiquee taught managerial finance, investment and portfolio management, and personal financial planning in the undergraduate program, and corporate finance and entrepreneurial finance in the MBA program. Dr. Siddiquee has developed and teaches a class, *A Master Class with Warren Buffett* in the summer. He is an avid value investor.

INDEX

www.ingramcontent.com/pod-product-compliance
Lightning Source LLC
Chambersburg PA
CBHW071302220526
45468CB00001B/236